Falling Through Space

THE JOURNALS OF

ELLEN GILCHRIST

BACK
BAY
BOOKS

Little, Brown & Company

Boston   New York   Toronto   London

FIRST PAPERBACK EDITION

Permissions to quote from copyright material appear on page 166.

Library of Congress Cataloging-in-Publication Data

Gilchrist, Ellen, 1935–
    Falling through space.

    1. Gilchrist, Ellen, 1935–   —Biography.
    2. Authors, American—20th century—Biography.
    I. Title.
PS3557.I34258Z465   1987   813'.54 [B]   87–3252
ISBN 0–316–31315–7 (hc)
ISBN 0–316–31317–3 (pb)

10 9 8 7 6 5

RRD-VA

Calligraphy by John W. Cataldo

DESIGNED BY JEANNE ABBOUD

*Published simultaneously in Canada
by Little, Brown & Company (Canada) Limited*

PRINTED IN THE UNITED STATES OF AMERICA

FALLING
THROUGH
SPACE

BY ELLEN GILCHRIST

FOR
MARSHALL AND ELLEN
AND AURORA

The Wu Li Masters know that "science" and "religion" are only dances, and that those who follow them are dancers. The dancers may claim to follow "truth" or claim to seek "reality" but the Wu Li Masters know better. They know that the true love of all dancers is dancing.

— Gary Zukav
from *The Dancing Wu Li Masters*

CONTENTS

ORIGINS

*T*HIS is my home. This is where I was born. This is the bayou that runs in my dreams, this is the bayou bank that taught me to love water, where I spent endless summer hours alone or with my cousins. This is where I learned to swim, where mud first oozed up between my toes. This is where I saw embryos inside the abdomens of minnows. This is where I believed that if I was vain and looked too long into the water I would turn into a flower.

This is where I learned the legend of the greedy dog. There was an old dog on a raft and he had a bone in his teeth and he looked down into the water and saw a dog carrying a bone and he dropped the one he was holding to snatch the other dog's bone away and so lost both bones, the real and the imaginary.

That's a new bridge. The one that was here when I was small had a beautiful elaborate scaffolding on top. I thought I must be a princess, of royal blood, to have such a bridge with such a magnificent top. To have such land with so many bugs and a bayou with so many fish and mussels and gars and maybe even alligators.

This is the porch that at one time ran all the way around the house. My grandfather built this house and my mother came here when she was four years old. My brother was born in that front bedroom. I was born forty miles away in a hospital and only came here three days later.

The ghost of Eli Nailor walks these halls. He was a black boy who was adopted by my great-great-grandmother when he was orphaned as a child. The woman I am named for raised him. He was the cook in this house all the days of his life and had a cabin beside the kitchen and the gardens and the henhouse and the chickenyard.

This was a good life. There were never slaves here. The
black people came here after the Civil War; they were free
people from Natchez. Black people and white people lived
and worked here in harmony. My grandfather thought of
himself as an Englishman. He was tall and proud and brave
and civilized.

Here is where my Aunt Roberta raised angora rabbits
during the Second World War and there is the chickenhouse
where I spied on the Broad Jump Pit when my brother and
my cousins were training for the Olympics.

This is the richest land in the world. The topsoil goes
thirteen to eighteen feet in some places. You could grow
anything here. We grew cotton. We grow soybeans also now.
My godfather, Coon Wade, farms this land. He was my
grandfather's friend. He serves that friendship still.

This is my world, where I was formed, where I came from,
who I am. This is where my sandpile was. I have spent a
thousand hours alone beneath this tree making forts for the
fairies to dance on in the moonlight. At night, after I was
asleep, my mother would come out here and dance her fingers
all over my sand forts so that in the morning I would see the
prints and believe that fairies danced at night in the sand.

This is where the barn used to be. There was a black
stallion here that we called the Count of Monte Christo and
mules so mean they could scare you out of riding them.

This is Ditty's cabin. She was as straight and tall as a tree,
half black and half white. She told the other black people
what to do. She was the mother of Mark and Inez and Man.
I would come here and ask permission to come in and she
would grant it and I would step over the wooden doorframe
to the dirt floor. I would sit on her bed, on her spotless
quilts, and eat cornbread and gossip about everything that
was going on.

Then I would go to the store and play the slot machine and

sell snuff and drink cold sweet drinks and eat pork and beans out of a can. Life is not supposed to be simple but it seemed simple to me. It was get up in the morning and be happy. It was go out in the yard and lie down on the ground and listen to China.

This is the levee. This is what keeps the Mississippi River within its banks. My father helped build this levee. I was conceived in a levee camp in a huge green tent from the Memphis tent company. In those photographs my mother is always wearing jodhpurs.

Before the white man came the Indians built mounds to get on when the water rose. Before even the Cherokees came the Mound Builders were here.

This is the Indian mound with a house built on top where my grandparents spent the first year of their marriage. There are other mounds on Hopedale Plantation. My great-grandmother forbade us to dig in them as they were sacred burial places. It was the only thing I ever remember Babbie forbidding us to do.

This was my great-great-grandmother's room. She lived until I was four in perfect health. When they used such things she would spend the late summer in this room sewing together the long white cotton bags the black people dragged behind them to pick the cotton.

These are the catfish ponds that take the place of cattle. Flying over my home I am appalled at how much of the land has been turned into catfish ponds. Things change. The only constant is change. There is nothing to fear. The land is its own God. It will heal itself if it needs to.

I could never live in a city. I need to smell the earth. I need to be here when it storms. At night when I was small great rainstorms would come swooping down across the Delta, tearing down the light poles and the telephone poles. My grandfather loved inventions. As soon as they invented the telephone he and his fellow planters met in Grace and arranged to have telephones. Then each of them cut down trees and strung wire and the wires met at the Grace post office and hooked up there to go to Rolling Fork and on to Greenville.

This is Greenfields' cemetery. This is where my mother's people are buried. Stewart Floyd Alford and Nell Biggs Alford and Margaret Connell and Ellen Martin and so forth and so on. My cousins and my friends.

I wish they had lived forever. This country was made by pioneers. They probably could not have imagined us, our numbers and our terrible problems, our crowded cities and wonderful medicines and bitter endless feuds. What will be happening fifty years from now that I cannot imagine? What will my great-great-grandchildren think of me when they walk in my house and read my books? When they try to piece together my life from my photographs and my legends.

THE ROAD to the store led past a line of pecan trees that looked down into the river. Swarms of gnats would come up out of nowhere and attack my face if I was stupid enough to walk there in the early morning or late afternoon. In the middle of the day the sun held them hostage on the bayou bank and I could walk along kicking the gravel with my sandals or stopping to pull up a dandelion or examine a rock or pause to feel my nickel in my pocket to make sure it was still there. Behind me Nailor and Baby Doll and Overflow and Henrietta were lined up on the porch stairs watching my progress. In front of m: the people sitting on the benches outside the store were already thinking of things to say to me. "Good morning, little missy, how you do today?" "Look out, here she comes, the girl that sells the snuff. How much you going to charge today for all your bags and cans?" "How about giving a few cans away?" "Look out for that dog. He's the king of fleas."

It was talk like music and it meant they liked me and thought that I was funny. I liked them too. I didn't have enough sense to know what it meant to be black. It never occurred to me that they might want to do a single thing they weren't already doing.

"I'm not putting this nickel in that hell-damn old slot machine today," I'd say, and go straight inside and stick it in and pull the handle. Two oranges and a bar. Three nickels for one. I stuck them in as fast as I could pull the handle. Then turned to my cousin Cincinnatus to see what he had for me to do.

"Lost your nickel already," he said, giggling from behind the cash register.

"I won three the first time," I answered. Yang and yin. I already knew the outcome was not the whole story of anything. I knew the end contains the beginning. In the strange way that children know everything because they forget nothing, I knew that the loss of a nickel to the judgment of the slot machine was nothing really, was only a way to get the damn smelly thing out of my hand. What was a nickel in the scheme of things? Buffalo on one side, White House on the other, made your hand smell funny to hold it and if you swallowed it you were dead. My uncle Robert had a framed picture in his doctor's office of all the things children had swallowed that he had retrieved. An open safety pin was the only one that really caught my eye.

So the nickel was gone as so many had gone before it and I was no less than I had been and still had the walk to the store, still had long cool baths in the tub that had been made especially for my grandfather, who was six feet four inches tall. A little girl could swim in that tub, could lie down and drown if no one was watching, but they were always watching, standing by with a hairbrush in their hands or sitting on a little stool and dripping water onto my back or begging me to let them wash my hair.

Dried with a big soft towel and carried down the hall and dressed in one of the beautiful soft cotton dresses they were always making me. My great-great-grandmother had been a milliner in Philadelphia and the women in that house were great artists of fashion and style and beauty. The clothes I wore when I was a child have spoiled me for life. At great collections in Paris or New York I turn up my nose at messy hems or anything that isn't French seamed or smocked by hand. When people ask me why there were so few women artists in the past, I tell them it's because their definition of artist is too narrow. I have worn dresses that should have won a Nobel. "Let me see that dress," everyone at the store would say. "Look here, Iris, see this dress Miss Babbie made this child." And their fingers would explore the rickrack or three-inch hem or perfectly fitted sleeves or smocking. Those artists did not have to wait for some stranger in New York to overcome his or her fear and say, Oh, yes, this is a nice piece of work. The audience and critics were right there in the room waiting for the last whir of the sewing machine and the moment when the dress would come down from the sewing table and be held up for inspection. What a life, with the sun pouring down outside on the richest land in the world. THE RICHEST LAND IN THE WORLD and we were happy there. The black people and white people worked together and spoke their grievances and only sickness or death or rain in September could make us sad. The days were long in that land of happy days and part of me lives there still.

A writer once said that a walk becomes a journey when there is a destination. I had a destination every afternoon when I was small. I would walk from the house to the store and if my nickel had to be sacrificed to my greed that was only one more gnat or interesting rock or possibly useful leaf.

℘

THE HARDEST THING to get hold of in the world is the truth; the easiest to keep once you capture it, once you know it plain. So I believe, but then I can't stand secrets. I want all the cards on the table. I want to know what's going on.

When I was a child I lived in a world of great order and politeness. "So polite," I once wrote, "that no one ever told the truth about anything." That was a cruel thing to write about a world as gentle and full of goodness as Hopedale Plantation. The grown people *were* elaborately and beautifully truthful about the surface of life, details, business arrangements, promises made and kept, appointments honored, facts kept straight. A man's word was his pledge in that world, his good name the dearest treasure of his life. Still, about the dark underside of life, birth and death, sex and the river, power and the wielding of power, God and the sky, these things stayed behind a levee of polite speaking and polite behavior. Why, when I was a child, did a certain pecan tree on the front lawn seem to have the greatest shadows and why was I the only one that ever played on the flagstone terrace beneath its branches or swung in its dusty web-covered swing? The grownups stayed away from that tree. With the great intuitive knowledge of children I knew I had that tree to myself. My cousins never played there. Even the wooden picnic table was never used and I would line up pecans upon its surface and make roads with them. The swing the rest of them used was one that swung out over the banks of the bayou. It was a nice swing also and anchored to a huge live oak tree, but no nicer than the pecan tree swing. As I said, I had that one to myself.

Many years later, on a cold fall day in Jackson, Mississippi, sitting in a car with my cousin, late in the afternoon, with

the sun almost gone from the sky, I began to talk about that
tree.

"It's still mysterious. And lonely. I went down there with
a film crew last month and they felt it. The land is so alive
down there."

"Perhaps it was the suicide?"

"What suicide?"

"A woman killed herself there. On that patio. Didn't you
know about that?"

"Who killed herself? What woman?"

"Someone they knew. She had cancer and she wouldn't
take whiskey for the pain. Nailor told me. She wouldn't take
whiskey or any kind of dope and so she killed herself instead.
At night beneath that tree."

"My God, the things that happened."

"I never would go near that tree after Nailor told me that."

"I wonder why no one ever told me?"

"Because you never listened. You were always talking."

"That's a nice thing to say."

"Well, it's true."

So the mystery was solved. And other mysteries open
before me. A mysterious world, only fifty years away.
Medical science was hard to practice when there were no
drugs, no real hope to offer. My great-uncle was the only
doctor in the county. He worked all day and read all night to
keep up with the advances in medical science. But there was
little he could do about things like cancer. When I first saw
Eugene Smith's beautiful photographic essay, "Country Doctor," I thought of Uncle Robert and wept for the mastery and
courage of his life. I should have wept for the time he had to
waste trying to give me typhoid shots. It would take hours of
pleading to get me to stick out my arm and hold still. Hours
of pleading and promises and sticks of peppermint candy and
being allowed to look at the skeleton in his closet. Afterwards
I would have to be put to bed for the afternoon to recover

from the trauma. I wonder what he did to recover from putting up with me.

The other great secret they kept from us was about sex. Whatever the animals did in the fields had nothing to do with what the white people did in the houses. The white people and beautiful tall sober black people who helped my grandfather run the place. *Nigger* was the word they used for black people who lived like animals. Nice people got married and were faithful and brought well-loved children into the world. At great danger to themselves women bore live children into the world that the world of men might live.

The graveyard around the little Episcopal church at Greenfields was littered with small tombstones that marked the graves of infants and children. It was hard to keep children alive in a land of mosquito-borne diseases. Children were bundled up and kept inside and watched over and guarded like diamonds. They were diamonds, black and white alike. Babies, new hope for the world, new voices in the clear blue air. Lambs were born in the pasture and colts and piglets and chickens hatched in the chickenyard and butterflies emerged from the cocoons we collected in the barn and calves dropped and all things multiplied and were fruitful in that rich fruitful land. Still, the birth of children was a thing apart. They were sent by God. Delivered by storks.

When I was nineteen years old, after having read thousands of books, on the night before I ran away to get married in the hills of north Georgia I sat up all night reading a book about how to have sexual intercourse. It was a book I had bought that afternoon at Rich's department store in Atlanta. I bought a white piqué dress with tiny pearl buttons all the way down the front. A white silk nightgown and robe, some white high-heeled shoes, and a book about sexual intercourse. That's how well the world in which I was born guarded the secret of sex.

* * *

I was contemptuous of that when I was young and cruel.
Now I am older and I think I understand what was going on.
It was how they protected us from being impregnated. They
didn't want that to happen to us. They didn't want us to
swell up with children and maybe die and begin the terrible
hard work of being mothers in a world where malaria flew in
the open screen doors or typhoid fever or yellow fever or
diphtheria or whooping cough or any of the terrible diseases
that filled the cemeteries while the land was being cleared
and the Mississippi Delta turned into farms, into a place
where people could live.

♈

I USED TO GO to the coast every Easter, to a frame house on a
peninsula beside a bayou that becomes a bay that runs into
the Gulf of Mexico at the exact point where the state of
Alabama meets the state of Florida. There were seven houses
on our peninsula. With pine trees and white sand beaches.
The sun shone like diamonds on the blue water and in the
early mornings dolphins came into the bayou and swam past
the pier in pairs, rolling and touching, pushing and caressing
each other with their snouts.

During the summer months the houses would be filled
with my cousins, but the place was deserted at Easter and I
would go there to be alone and think things over at the point
where winter meets spring in my imagination. Well, not
really alone for I would have my children with me. But
almost never my husband, as I was usually "separated" from
him. I was young and confused during those years and I

would run home to my parents every time another child was born.

So it would be Easter and I would be alone on the coast. It is still cold there that time of year and I would lie in the sun covered with Bain de Soleil and goose bumps and read the *Four Quartets* out loud to myself while my wild redheaded children fought and built fires and collected firewood and drank Cokes and dyed eggs and wrote on themselves with ball-point pens and turned their backs the color of sunsets from bending over on the beach to build castles.

The *Four Quartets*. Thomas Stearns Eliot's great paean to the days of Easter. "Burnt Norton," "East Coker," "The Dry Salvages," "Little Gidding."

> *Home is where one starts from. As we grow older*
> *The world becomes stranger, the pattern more complicated . . .*

I would look up from my book, too young to know what all that meant. Too easily influenced to know there are other ways to grow old, that it can mean having the world grow simpler, clearer, more beautiful, less complicated. I would look down the beach. The children would be tearing into the sand with their shovels, launching their homemade kites, hauling up crab traps with their long, skinny, amazingly strong arms. They were all good swimmers. I never worried about them near the water. The real danger at Cotton Bayou was from the sun.

"You better get a shirt on," I would call out. "Or put on some suntan lotion. It won't be my fault if you get burned. Don't come crying to me when your skin falls off."

"As soon as we're finished," they would call back. "As soon as we get through."

"All right," I'd say. "I warned you. Don't say I didn't warn you." I would return to my book.

> *Time present and time past*
> *Are both perhaps present in time future,*

And time future contained in time past.
If all time is eternally present
All time is unredeemable.
What might have been is an abstraction . . .

"Momma," someone would cry out. "Marshall spit at me.
Marshall and Garth said they're going to drown me."

"He got some wood from under the Johnstons' house,"
another voice would yell. "He stole the Johnstons' firewood."

"I did not. Besides, he stole my crabs. He let my crabs
go."

"I did not!! Besides, the crabs belong to everybody. All the
crabs are everyone's in the world."

"Momma said if I put out the crab traps the crabs were
mind. *Didn't you, Momma. Didn't you say the crabs were mine!!*"

"Why don't you go in the house and get some Cokes," I
would advise. "Get out the Hershey's and make some fudge
for lunch. And leave me alone a minute, won't you. Can't
you see I'm studying poetry?"

The concert would subside.

The Coke brigade would file past me up the stairs. I would
return to Eliot.

Footfalls echo in the memory
Down the passage which we did not take
Towards the door we never opened . . .

Four Quartets. Maundy Thursday, Good Friday, Holy
Saturday, Easter Sunday. The days slipped through my hands
like music while the children's backs grew redder, the supply
of Cokes smaller, the piles of wet clothes higher.

Sometimes other divorcées and their children went with us
to the coast. The women and I would walk the lonely beaches
talking about the men we had married and failed to love and
stolen the lovely sunburned children from. We were full of
brittle justifications. We could not figure out what had gone
wrong. We had been so beautiful and gifted and polite. We

had meant so well. There had been so much of everything. How could we be unhappy? How could we be alone?

The coast was a refuge for us during those hard years, a place of healing and reflection. We would walk the beaches together like women whose men have gone to war. Beside us the great pounding heart of the ocean, the sea breeze in our hair, the voices of our children rising and falling in the distance. We would walk the beaches and tell our stories until they assumed the qualities of myths. . . . "Momma," a child's voice would call out from behind a sand dune. . . . "I found a sandpiper's nest. . . . I found a cowrie shell. . . . I found a conch. . . . I found a red triton and Marshall says it's his. . . ."

MY COUSIN Bubba Finley was a genius. He was the first boy in Issaquena County to build a radio that could talk to foreign countries. He talked to England and Australia and France and Mexico and the Caribbean islands.

Picture a two-story frame house beside a lake. There is a huge magnolia tree right in the middle of the front yard and screened-in porches around three sides. There is a parlor as big as a dance hall but no one ever goes into it except Bubba's twin sister, Laura. She goes in to practice the piano. Many rooms surround the parlor, going out in all directions, bedrooms, kitchens, halls. My aunt Roberta and cousin Nell are out in the yard practicing cheerleading in their heavy white wool sweaters. It is August and hot as the gates of hell but they have to wear them to get used to them for the fall. I want to be them more than anything in the world but I am not. I am ten years old and I'm spending the week at Onnie Maud's house as a reward for being reasonable about my typhoid shot. Life is good.

It is midmorning, let us say, and Laura is in the parlor playing *Clair de lune*. Across the road is Lake Washington, the biggest cypress swamp in the world, mysterious and beautiful in the morning sun. It is a lake left behind when the Mississippi River changed its course and went to Greenville.

Onnie Maud's husband, Doctor Finley, is in his brick office across the street giving shots and showing his skeleton to children and telling ladies when their babies will come and waiting for an emergency. At any moment a mule will step on someone's foot or someone will break a bone or get bit by a dog and have to have rabies shots or step on a rusty nail and need a tetanus shot. I have seen them drag suffering victims up onto Onnie Maud's porch right in the middle of Doctor Finley's Sunday afternoon nap. The atmosphere hushed and dangerous and afraid. He would rise from his bed. It seemed as if he slept in his suit. He would take the victim into his hands. No wonder his son turned into a mechanical genius. Not that the radio was the only way Bubba's genius manifested itself. He also had an unbelievable tenor voice with a huge range. He would lie out in the backyard sunning his lungs, then rise up and go about the halls, singing at the top of his voice.

I adored him. I adored him more than his piano-playing twin sister, or his wonderful older sister, Nell, or more than Onnie Maud herself, with her unerring ability to make a ten-year-old girl look like a princess by the application of a curling iron and Laura Finley's beautiful hand-me-down pinafores and dresses. Talk about genius! How those women could sew.

The first time I made one of these broadcasts for National Public Radio I thought of Bubba. I was in New York City with earphones on my ears talking to Bob Edwards in Washington. A wonderful red-haired girl named Manoli Wetherall was in the control booth. There were soft white things on the walls reminiscent of the egg cartons Bubba used to line his room. I was enormously at home in that place. I felt as if I had been there before and I trusted it to be a place that was on a quest for truth, the only journey I am interested in going on. This is a writer's journal. You must understand how significant these relationships and correspondences seem to me. How I rely on them to tell me what to do next and where to go and who to trust in the world.

CP

I RECEIVED a letter the other day from a woman in England. She loved my stories and sent me word that they made her want a mayonnaise sandwich and a Coke with a hole in the top of the cap. The letter was sent through my agent. It was part of a letter she wrote to him thanking him for sending her my books. She is the wife of one of his English authors but was raised in the American South.

"A mayonnaise sandwich and a Coke with a hole in the top?" my agent asked. "What is this strange southern meal? I have asked everyone in our office and even our resident Georgian cannot shed light on this menu."

Here is what I wrote in reply. *Dear Michael,* I wrote,

A long time ago people lived in houses where there was a constant supply of babies who drank out of baby bottles. I was fortunate to live in such a house and had baby bottles available to me anytime I wanted one so I never had to resort to the common practice of putting a hole in the cap of a Coca-Cola bottle with an icepick and sucking out the Coke.

I have, however, tasted this drink and it is indescribable, a combination of cola and cork and tin, and maybe even lead, dangerous and wild.

Part II. Mayonnaise sandwich. Take a loaf of white bread. Discard the ends. Eat a piece. Take two other pieces. Lay them flat on a plate. Open a jar of mayonnaise or Kraft Miracle Whip. Put as much mayonnaise as possible on each piece. Push the pieces together. Bon appetit.

Of such moments are the rewards of a writer's life concocted. The unfortunate part is that life imitates art so enthusiastically in my case at least that the minute I write down anything as seductive as the words *mayonnaise sandwich* I have to go and eat one. I always do it sooner or later — it might be days later — but what I generally do is go on and eat whatever it is right then and get it over with.

This is more than I need to know about the effect of thought upon action.

꼭

I FOUND a note to myself on the back of a tablet this morning. Get back to that happy child lying in the yard in front of the house listening to China. That's what the note said. What it meant was, go back into the self, not the thousand masquerades I am so adept at assuming. Back to that warm fat little girl lying on the grass in front of my grandmother's house, with the grass scratching my legs and the smell of the earth and its incredible richness.

The bayou was going by not a hundred yards away but I was not listening to the bayou. I was listening to China. Right underneath me were thousands of Chinese people hurrying through the streets of their crowded cities, carrying marvelous paper umbrellas, pulling each other in carts, endlessly polite and smiling.

Meanwhile, right there in Issaquena County, Mississippi, I was in a house full of people who were also being very polite to each other, on the surface, but underneath was China, exciting undercurrents, alliances, power and usurpations of power, statements and allegations and rumors. This was not black against white or anything as mundane as that. No, this was Onnie Maud in Glen Allen having allegedly made the statement that Miss Teddy was grieving too long over her dead husband and visiting his grave too often.

My great-grandmother, Babbie, and Eli Nailor, the cook, were staying in the kitchen trying to keep out of it, but they kept being drawn into the fray. I hung out in the kitchen all I could in those days, as close as possible to the pantry where they kept the pinch cakes, long trays of yellow cake that we were allowed to break pieces off of in between meals, so I was spending a lot of time on a stool by the pantry anyway and got to hear everything that was going on.

There were German prisoners of war working the fields of Hopedale Plantation that summer and there was fighting in Europe and the Pacific and we heard reports of that every day at noon on the radio. But the war that interested me was the one that was raging between the big house and the house on Lake Washington where Onnie Maud lived with her husband, Uncle Robert, who was the only doctor for miles around. Onnie Maud was supposed to have said that about Teddy and a cousin in Rolling Fork had reported it and Teddy wanted to go up to Glen Allen and confront Onnie Maud and get it over with but my grandmother was against it and thought they should let sleeping dogs lie. The reason Miss Teddy's husband had died in the first place was because he was trying to save the levee, and she was only twenty-six years old at the time and pregnant and she thought she should get to grieve as long as she wanted to. Who was Onnie Maud to criticize her grief, up there in Glen Allen with her doctor husband in perfect health?

All that summer they would come into the kitchen one at a time and try to get my great-grandmother and Nailor to take sides but they wouldn't do it. Neither would I. I just kept on getting all the pinch cake I could and Nailor kept sitting on his chair saying this too shall pass away and my great-grandmother kept on making the mayonnaise. She would drop the Wesson Oil one drop at a time into the lemon and the egg, then beat it with the whip.

"What makes it mayonnaise?" I would ask.

"It's a colloid," she would answer. "Doctor Finley says it's a colloid."

I would stare off into the pantry, filled with the mystery of mayonnaise. Of course, this was a long time ago when people lived in houses where a lot was going on, and China was only the speed of dreams away.

I AM heavily under the influence this morning of a movie called *The Gods Must Be Crazy,* about a family of African bushmen in Botswana. These bushmen never say a cross word to their children and the children grow up to be the sweetest, gentlest, most lighthearted people in the world. Sir Laurens Van Der Post writes about these people, in books with wonderful names like *The Mantis Prayer,* and *The Lost World of the Kalihari* and *The Heart of the Hunter.*

I'm a sort of bushman. My mother never said a cross word to me. Even when she would pretend to discipline me, when she would knit her brows and screw up her lips and try to bring a little order into my life, I knew she didn't have her heart in it. I knew she thought it was funny as all get-out that I was wild and crazy. She still thinks it's funny.

She'd fit right in with those bushmen. She's got this gift of knowing that life is supposed to be a happy outrageous business. "Let's go shopping," that's her idea of how to discipline an unruly child. "I think you need some new shoes."

I almost never went to school. That's why I'm a writer. Anytime I wanted to I could wake up and say I was sick and she'd let me stay home and read books. If she came into my room I'd start turning the pages real slowly as if I was barely able to lift the book, or I'd clutch my stomach or my head. She would bring me cool drinks and bathe my face with a warm cloth and around noon she'd show up with a sickbed tray, chopped steak and mashed potatoes and baked apples dyed green, one of her specialties.

Then, when it was afternoon and too late to get sent back to school, I'd recover and get dressed and go outside and get in my treehouse and finish my book. I was reading about ten or twelve a week at that time. The stars on my reading chart fell off the board and dripped down onto the floor.

I really think this bushman stuff has a lot to do with my being a writer. I'm doing the same thing right this very minute that I did in the third grade. I'm all alone in a bedroom with some cookies and a drink, surrounded by books. When I get through for the day, when I recover, I'll get dressed and go down to town and see what's going on.

Why have I been doing this? What have I been trying to find out all these long years of my extended bushman childhood? What am I hoping to learn from all this character and scene and plot? I don't know. All I know for sure is that by this means, ever since I was a small child, every now and then I'd get a glimpse, like a shiver, of what's underneath the illusion, and it's the promise of another look at that that drives me to do this absurd thing for a living. An intimation of something wonderful and light, a chance to see what's really going on, stars and subatomic particles and so forth.

That's the thing that wakes me at dawn and keeps me in this room while everyone else is out in the real world making deals and talking on the phone and running the place.

We live at the level of our language. Whatever we can articulate we can imagine or understand or explore. All you have to do to educate a child is leave him alone and teach him to read. The rest is brainwashing.

I HAVE BEEN moving around all my life. Going to different schools, living in different houses, shedding old roles, assuming new ones. This way of life is as natural to me as staying in one place is for other people. I do variations on the theme. I return to places where I used to be. I find my old personas. I try them on. If they still fit, I wear them out to a party or a show. If they begin to restrict my movements, I take them off. I am a human being, capable of mimicking anything I see or remember or can imagine. This week I am in the middle of moving back to Jackson, Mississippi. Finding my old friends. I am the hunter home from the hills, with stories to tell, news to catch up on, compliments to exchange.

I began my roaming life during the Second World War — every five or six months I moved to a new town and went to a new school. Some children are harmed by this process. I thrived on it. My parents are stable and enthusiastic people. A war had to be won and we were part of winning it. What had to be done would be done. I was raised to believe that people are brave and resourceful and resilient.

Now, here I am, so many years later, sitting in an empty apartment waiting for my furniture to arrive and I am perfectly happy and I have this wild idea that I know exactly what I'm doing and am in charge of my own destiny. I see myself as deliberately playing out an old scenario from my childhood. Tearing up a perfectly nice comfortable life and going off to live somewhere else. Deliberately complicating things.

Well, I am a writer and when life becomes comfortable for an artist the energy stops — nothing in the long history of our species has prepared us to be comfortable. Being comfortable is so boring it makes us drink and take drugs and bet on football games. Anything for a little excitement, so I invented this adventure for myself. My belongings are somewhere on a moving van between Fayetteville, Arkansas, and Jackson, Mississippi. My papers are scattered everywhere. My mind is like a pile of pick-up sticks, seeing new streets, new trees, new faces, learning my new address and phone number.

I wish I knew what I was really up to. A writer's mind is as full of tricks as a magician's. I might be running away from wondering if my new book is any good. I might wake up a year from now and decide this whole thing was either absolutely sane or absolutely crazy.

꼬

MY GRANDCHILDREN are visiting me. Marshall Walker, age four, and Ellen Walker, age one — and I am watching the terrible pangs of sibling rivalry. This is real suffering and all I ever need to know about jealousy, its power and its source.

For a whole year Marshall has put up with this baby hanging on his mother and sucking on her breasts and sleeping in her arms. He has put up with her walking into his room and picking up his toys and getting all the attention.

But my house on the mountain is another thing. I am his grandmother. I belong to him, hook, line, and sinker. My piano belongs to him and my closet full of toys and my chairs and my pillows and my bed. Also, the box of huge wooden blocks a friend of mine always brings over when she knows he's coming.

Now this one-year-old baby girl is actually walking around this place touching anything she wants to touch. This is the first time she has been here since she could walk. He is going crazy. He sobbed himself to sleep the first night he was here, exhausted from trying to protect his territory. I am in such sympathy with him I have found myself taking sides against my own little granddaughter. These lessons are too hard to learn. This is more than I want to know about jealousy.

Be objective, I kept saying to myself. Then he would sit down to play the piano and here she would come, beating on the bass keys, ruining his music. Be objective, I warned myself. Then he began building a spaceship out of the blocks. He had been working for an hour stacking and arranging them, humming happily to himself as he formed the cockpit, the wings, the fuselage. She came walking out of the kitchen and destroyed half a wing with a sweep of her hand. He was on top of her in an instant. He grabbed her

I will find some light at the end. Remember the wonderful scene when she goes at night to her workshop, certain she has failed, and then sees the light shining from the petri dish? That's the sort of fantasy that leads me on.

I refuse to be cynical in any way about my work. My work helps me live my life. It tells me who I am. Take *The Annunciation,* for example — my so-called novel. What was that obsession with adoption about? I'm not adopted and I've never given a child away. Was it about my son in Alaska? When my middle son was eighteen, he handed me a high school diploma, got into a pickup truck, and drove up the Alaska highway to Fairbanks to work on the pipeline. He was happy as a lark, doing exactly what he wanted to do.

Meanwhile I was down in New Orleans, going crazy, staying up nights with outdoors catalogs, ordering triple-lined down coats and gloves and helmets guaranteed to work in the Antarctic and flare kits and sending them to him. I must have sent him half a dozen flare kits. Every day that child was in Alaska I would wake up and wonder if his eyeballs had frozen yet. He didn't even have a phone. I couldn't even call him up. It's not easy being a mother. It never ends. The child grows up and the mother keeps on mothering. It's pitiful. It drives you crazy. It drives you to write novels about adoption.

A critic once wrote to me and said, Ellen, for God's sake stop writing novels for therapy. It was good advice but how can I stop?

Anyway, my son didn't freeze to death in Alaska — he made a lot of money and spent it and learned how to take tractors apart and came home and got married and now he's farming in north Mississippi and I don't have to order any more flare kits or write any more books about lost children. Now I can go back to work writing about people who are looking for love in all the wrong places.

head in his hands. His mouth was open. I leaped over a st
of books. "Don't bite," I screamed. "Did he bite her?"
mother asked. "No," I said. "I stopped it. Come on,'
added, grabbing him up. "Let's get out of here." We we
out to the shed and found our old green tent and set it u
under a maple tree and spread some sleeping bags on th
ground and put the blocks on them and got a radio and pu
it in the window of the shed attached to fifty feet of extensio
cord and turned on KUAF's "Jazz and Fusion Hour." W
have moved to the yard.

A psychiatrist friend suggests that the best thing to do is
to show him the world is big and full of more exciting things
than his mother's breasts. I agree. We're going to build
telephones from the tent to the shed and start some swimming lessons and as soon as he gets home this afternoon I am
going to call my older brother and apologize to him for being
alive.

<p>

THESE JOURNAL ENTRIES allow me to answer questions reporters
ask me about my work. I am always dissatisfied with the
reports that reach my readers. The boring little domestic
details of my life don't seem to have anything to do with the
mental life that makes the stories, with the real excitement of
writing, the pitchblende I refine in search of radium. I'm so
influenced by movies I saw as a child that that is actually how
I view what I'm doing. I think of myself as a sort of literary
Madame Curie in a shed in Paris surrounded by tables piled
high with pitchblende. If I keep on trying, if I do the work,

My little redheaded grandchild has become very conscious of his hair. He fills the sink with water, then pulls a chair up to it, then very carefully, for he is a careful and precise child, he dips the top of his head down into the water. He looks in the mirror and smooths the sides down, then pushes up a small piece in the back.

"What have you done to your hair?" his mother said when she first noticed it. "It is the chicken look," he said. "I am the chicken style."

I suppose it was inevitable that sooner or later I must tell you about the overpowering joy of being a grandparent. People try to make light of this relationship. They say it is because a grandparent can give a child back to its parents when she becomes tired of caring for it. Not true.

His name is Marshall, this little boy that I adore. He has brown eyes and a wonderful large nose like Albert Einstein's and large ears like the Gautama Buddha's and I am sick at the thought that he must ever go to school. How awesome that one woman should have twenty or thirty children to care for all day. How could she help but make mistakes? Something is wrong at the very basis of our ideas about schools.

"The chicken look," he said. "I am the chicken style."

Last week I was down in Jackson, Mississippi, with my grandchild. I had taken him to visit my mother, that famous child-worshipper. We had Marshall, age three, and his cousin Heather, age four, and we had been at it with them for about twenty-four hours. I had them in the business of filling up a birdbath using eight-ounce plastic glasses. The birdbath is on the back of the yard in a bed of daffodils and the source of water is beside the house. About ten minutes of absolute peace had gone by. They were robotlike in their dedication to the idea of helping birds. I was feeling very powerful having hit upon this great idea to get them to leave me alone. I wanted to write about it. To describe the self-satisfied look on their faces as they filled the cups and carried them carefully back across the yard and dumped them in. What good citizens, helping the birds. I wanted to write about it but I didn't dare begin. I knew what would happen. The minute I got involved in my work they would sense I had stopped watching them and come running. I stood there thinking about what it would be like to be a young mother trying to write or paint or do anything alone in a house with small children. And yet life without them would be meaningless to me.

A poet told me that when her little boys were small she used to put her typewriter in the playpen and sit there and work while they tore up the house around her. Of course, she is an exceptionally energetic and resourceful person.

MY FOUR-YEAR-OLD GRANDSON and I were uninvited guests the other morning at the wedding of Sharon James to Jacob Clayton. It was a wedding in a castle. Along with my recent campaign to cure him of sibling rivalry, I have been taking Marshall out to explore the world. This being a Saturday we left early and stopped by the Station to pick up some muffins and then, carrying our boxes, we walked down to Wilson Park to eat breakfast in the castle.

The castle is a strange thing, rising up from the ground beside a creek that runs by the baseball diamond. It was built in 1979 by a sculptor named Frank Williams and was paid for by the National Endowment for the Arts. Frank employed CETA workers and at one time or another two dozen young people worked on the project, learning to mix concrete and lay stones and divert water, learning useful skills while they created magic.

The result is a real castle, built of stone and concrete, with a throne room and turrets and a bridge and towers that are inlaid with runes and small art objects and tiles bearing symbols both sacred and scary.

I had lunch at the castle on my forty-fifth birthday. But I had never been there for breakfast. Marshall and I arrived with our boxes and found the place packed with people wearing tuxedos. Sharon James and Jacob Clayton had hit upon the idea of getting married beside the moat.

There were bridesmaids in pink cotton, a bride in white lace who looked sixteen and not a day older. A three-tier wedding cake made by Josephine Banks, and a flower girl named Janie who emerged from her mother's car wearing pale pink and long gold ringlets. Marshall went crazy when he saw her and started flexing his muscles and making his motorcycle engine noise.

"I am never getting married," he said, when she had disappeared down the aisle beside the ring bearer. "I'm going to be an artist and paint and paint and paint."

Marshall is going through a difficult, highly critical, and generally unattractive phase right now. "Besides," he added, "it's going to rain."

I looked up. He was right. Rain clouds were gathering. Rain was on its way. But the preacher had begun the ceremony. He was already to the part about in sickness and in health and forsaking all others. The bride stared straight ahead. The maid of honor scratched her arm with a lace glove. I pulled Marshall's wonderful strong little body into my own and thought about the day his grandfather and I ran away to the hills of north Georgia to be married by a justice of the peace with a sheriff in attendance. We weren't much older than the children being married by this moat. Because of that this little boy exists and my middle age is charmed and rich and full of laughter.

"When are they going to eat the cake?" he asked, pretending to have lost interest in the flower girl.

"I was thinking of making some cakes this afternoon," I answered. "A pineapple upside-down cake and a marble cake and some cupcakes with colored icing. You want to help me do it?"

"Let's go," he said. "Let's go get started."

℘

I'VE BEEN UP in Chickasaw County, Mississippi, watching a house being moved down the Natchez Trace. My son, Garth Walker, and his wife, Jean Verrell, have taken it upon themselves to move a hundred-year-old house from downtown Houston, Mississippi, five miles out the Trace to Jeannie's farm. The weather has not been propitious for this undertaking. First there was rain, now there is snow. But my brave children are going right along with their plans. As of yesterday, half of the house (it had to be cut in two) had come to rest underneath a circle of oak trees and the other half will be moved today.

Jeannie's farm is on land that people in Chickasaw County call the Horsenation, a plateau where the Confederate Army hid its horses during the Civil War. Later, when the war was over, it was the site of many famous rodeos.

I watched the first half of the house being moved. I drove up the Trace and got to Houston just in time to see the house coming down the main street on a flatbed truck. Two men were standing on top moving power lines out of the way, and everyone in town had come out of their houses and stores to watch the progress.

Traffic was stopped for an hour in the middle of town, but no one seemed to mind. They have known Jeannie and her family a long time and if she wants to buy an old house and move it to her farm it's okay with them. Any tree branches that were in the way were cheerfully cut down and thrown to the side. This is rich and fertile land with many trees and no one minds losing a branch or two.

The house proceeded down the main street and turned onto Highway 389 and on down to the entrance to the Trace. My son was standing on the overpass with the park ranger. They were discussing the tendency of certain overprotective mothers to come driving up the Trace to make sure a house doesn't fall on anyone.

I watched the house move up the ramp and turn left onto the Trace. A chandelier in a bedroom swung gaily on its chain and I thought, Someday I'll be sleeping in one of those bedrooms holding a grandchild in my arms and I'll be telling him or her about the time I watched his house being moved along the Natchez Trace to his mother's farm.

I thought too of the Temple of Dendur in the Metropolitan Museum of Art in New York City, which was moved stone by stone from a little port on the Nile River to a glass-covered room on Fifth Avenue.

Man and his dreams, Stonehenge and the Great Wall of China and the Temple of Dendur and the Pyramids. The urge to civilization is to conquer or to build.

As I was trying to remember the rest of that quotation my son's house passed the Aberdeen exit and disappeared into the trees.

☿

IN THE LONG HOT SUMMERS of my so-called youth I used to put on plays. I put them on in treehouses and on porches and in basements. Basements were the best. In the first place they were cool, in the second place they were mysterious, and in the third place there was always a coal bin that the actors could use for a dressing room.

The most memorable play I produced was in the basement of a house in Harrisburg, Illinois. My co-director was Cynthia Jane Hancock, who would grow up to become a head cheerleader and drum majorette and, later, a finalist for Mrs. Illinois. She was made for the stage. I, alas, was not.

This particular performance was a variety show. Cynthia, dressed as Wonder Woman, would tap dance to "Meet Me in Saint Louis." Dressed as Cat Woman, I would follow her singing "The Desert Song." Our audience consisted of six or seven neighborhood children and the son of the Harrisburg newspaper editor. He was there with his camera, ready to record for all time the premiere performance of *The Main Street Review*.

It was ten o'clock on a Saturday morning in the very heart of July. The audience was seated on a line of old footlockers. The show began. Cynthia stepped up on the wooden stage and wowed them with her rendition of "Meet Me in Saint Louis." They screamed for more. She did "East Side, West Side" and left the stage with a curtsy and a bow. It was my turn. My Cat Woman costume was a green one-piece bathing suit with a gold cummerbund and a black hat. I stepped up on the stage. I opened my mouth to sing. It was my favorite song. I had sung it a thousand times. Blue Heaven, I began. Blue Heaven, Blue Heaven. What was next? I could not remember. No words came. Blue Heaven, I began again. The audience waited politely. They ate their popcorn and drank their Cokes. I tried again. Blue Heaven. Blue Heaven and You and I. Blue Heaven. The audience looked down at the floor. I can't do it, I said. I can't remember the words. Cynthia stood up. I guess the show is over, she said. You can go home now if you want to.

I HAVEN'T HAD a vacation from writing in ten years. Ever since the afternoon in 1975 when I pulled my old portable typewriter out of a closet and went off to the Caicos Islands to write poetry, I've been writing or wishing I was writing every single day from dawn to noon.

Now, suddenly, the spell is broken and I've been wildly happy for three weeks — first I lost six pounds. Then I bought some makeup. Then I decided to move back to Mississippi into the bosom of my wild, beautiful family.

Don't get cocky and think you can go home again, a friend warned me. Well, I'm going home anyway. If my father wants to get up in the middle of the night and argue with me about the Federal Reserve system, I'm ready.

If my grandchildren boss me around unceasingly, I'm ready. If I have to fight for everything I've struggled to learn and believe in, I'm ready.

Because I miss the state of Mississippi with its wonderful fields and trees and rivers and bright-eyed imaginative children.

Fayetteville, Arkansas, has been good to me. The quiet beauty of the Ozark Mountains has given me the strength to write three books of fiction and a book of poems and a play.

Now it's time to go home to the real material. To the place where I was born and the beautiful musical language that I first learned to speak. What you hear on the radio is only a ghost of those long vowel sounds. It is a language that's more like singing than like talking. So I'm going home. I'll fly back to Fayetteville and start packing up my papers and closing my little house on the mountain where I tried to be a slave to literature. That didn't work out for me.

I kept thinking about a poem by Louis Simpson called "The Springs of Gadera" about a man in publishing who dreams he is pushing a huge stone around a circle. One day he kicks his desk drawer shut and gets up and walks out. He looks back over his shoulder and imagines he sees some other poor guy pushing the same stone around the same old worn-out circular path. As for me, I'm tired of being a nun to art. I'm going to go live in the capital city of the state of Mississippi and find out what's going on in the modern world.

$\mathcal{P}$

I CAN BARELY remember the Thanksgivings of my life. They fade into the late fall whiteness between Halloween and Christmas and there they lie, lost and forgotten or awash in a sea of rice and gravy and white meat. I never did like to eat dinner with large groups of people. I am more the type to take a sandwich up into a tree and nibble around the crust while I read.

The one Thanksgiving that I do remember was one in which I created something. At that time my parents lived on a farm in Rankin County, Mississippi, and my brothers and my three sons and my six nieces were there all the time anyway, so coming to Summerwood for Thanksgiving was nothing new. It was a wonderful creative time in my life. My parents were helping take care of my children. I was back in school at Millsaps College. Life was good. The children were still small enough to be manageable and I was writing and studying philosophy.

That Thanksgiving I decided to turn the day into a family Olympics. We marked off courses and had three-legged races and sprints and throwing contests and a steeplechase that consisted of a long course around the farm, over the dam, through the woods, around a barn, up and down hills, over a fence, and down a gravel road to a tent underneath an oak tree. I had been running quite a bit that fall and I am sure the driving motivation in my mind was that I would surprise and conquer my older brother, who once came in third in the real Junior Olympics. I have forgotten what came of that. I think he refused to race. Or else he raced but didn't try and infuriated me by letting me win. When we were small, one of my greatest complaints was that he let me win. "YOU LET ME WIN," I would scream, "YOU LET ME WIN. I HATE YOU." "Don't hate anyone," my mother would whisper.

Still, it was a wonderful day and we resolved to make the races an annual event. Two of my nieces were moved to write a newsletter about the day, which they copied on the office copying machine and sent around to the participants. That was so long ago. In 1967.

Recently one of the young editors found a copy and mailed it off to everyone who had been there for the first running of the Summerwood Thanksgiving Olympics. It was full of interesting interviews with the participants.

"My foot got hurt but I had fun anyway." Kathleen Gilchrist. "Tremendous success." Uncle Bob. I am quoted as saying, "Lovely healthy children are the greatest blessing of any year." And I might add from the perspective of 1986, especially when someone else is taking care of them most of the time.

℘

I KNOW SO MUCH MORE now than I knew then, except for a very
long time ago, when I knew everything. I knew it all, where
the barn was and how to ride the mules and where they kept
the pound cake and how far to walk into the water without
drowning, the smell of coffee and powder, the breasts of
Babbie and Dan-Dan and Miss Teddy and Onnie Maud, the
cold hands of Nailor. The soft bones of my mother, the bed
of Aunt Roberta, how to get all the sugar I wanted, the way
to Hannie's house and where the men had gone and why the
women stopped what they were doing when the news came
over the radio about the war.

Later, I would ride in the crop duster and be pulled on a
board behind the motorboat and drive the new Buick around
the pasture and wear slips that came from Memphis in boxes
lined with pale pink tissue paper. I would grow up without
noticing it since I had never thought that I was a child or
seemed helpless or small to myself in any way.

I feared water unless they were with me and darkness and
underneath the beds. I was afraid I would go rolling down
the bayou bank in the car and forget to roll the windows up
or down, whichever it was that saved your life. I was afraid
I would be turned into a crow for lying, so I told the truth.
Some of them regret teaching me that.

The black children came over in the morning to play with
me. We played on the back porch and on the stairs behind
the kitchen. We made doll furniture and chattered away in
two languages. Their language was full of laughter. Mine was
full of bossiness and warnings. I made the furniture and they
admired it and ate the pound cake I got from the pantry and
when it was gone they left. They wearied of watching me
work so hard over nothing on such beautiful mornings with
the ground so soft and fragrant beneath our feet. They would

thank me very politely for the cake, then disappear. When they were gone I would put on my shoes and walk down the road searching for them. I would go to Ditty's house and ask her to find them for me. She would give me cornbread and let me watch her make spells. She was very good at making spells. She must have put a spell on me for me to be so lucky all my life. Yes, it must have been Ditty. For love of my mother she must have covered me with spells.

When we were away from Hopedale, sometimes for many months, I would write letters to them. Mrs. Stewart Floyd Alford, Hopedale Plantation, Grace, Mississippi.

In my imagination the mailman would drive his car down the gravel road from the Grace post office, past the Indian mounds and on past my godmother's house, past the shed where the crop dusters were parked and over the Hopedale Bridge and along the pasture where my grandfather's sheep grazed. He would stop the car and walk up onto the porch and hand the letter to my grandmother.

Dear Dan-Dan [the letter would say],

How are you? I am well. Danny died. He was run over and I stayed under the bed all day and would not come out. It is cold in Indiana but we like it here. Daddy has an A gas ration sticker and on Sundays we ride around in the car. We went to see some apple orchards and some goats. I will be there as soon as I can. Make some pound cakes and tell everyone I am coming. Your granddaughter, Ellen.

Dear Babbie,

Thanks for the letter with the good advice. I have read so many books there is no room for stars on my chart. I read about four a day and I am writing letters to everyone in Hollywood and everywhere we have been. We are rolling stones now, Daddy says. He says not to worry. Who wants to gather moss but mother wants to.

She says it drives her crazy to pack all the time. I don't care what happens as long as Dooley doesn't come in my room. He is spoiled rotten. They love him more than they love me, but you like me just as much, don't you? Granny doesn't like me at all compared to him. She only likes boys. Yours very truly, Your great-granddaughter, Ellen.

Dear Cousin Nell,

We are all so sorry your husband died. We cried and cried when the letter came. Please come and stay with us. You can sleep in my room. I hate to sleep there by myself. It won't help much but you have to do something. You can't stay in Glen Allen and grieve. I love you so much. You are my favorite person in the world. Yours most sincerely, Cousin Ellen.

I will do anything in the world to make you feel better. I have a new Jantzen bathing suit. It's two-piece.

Dear God,

I will never believe in you again for making Floyd die and Nell's husband and putting Dooley's eye out. You can count on this. I will never believe in you again because I didn't to begin with and I will spit on the floor if they make me go to church and kneel. I hate your guts. Who are you to make people die? I'm not going to. I'm going to be a vampire and live in the basement. If you are real strike me dead for writing this. See, you are a damn hell damn hell damn. Goddamn, Goddamn. It's going to be my favorite word. Yours very truly, Ellen Louise Gilchrist, September 1943.

Dear Diary,

This is the worst summer of my life. Floyd died and Dooley put out his eye and Momma is having a baby and we can't even go to Hopedale. The good part is the war is about over and the lady next door gave me a dressing table with doors that swing in and out. I am going to cover it with movie star pictures as soon as I get time. There is a gold star on the door across the street and a gold star on Mrs. Mattingly's house and some of my teeth are coming out. I hope to have better news for you the next time I write. Yours very truly, Ellen Leigh. (I changed my name.)

Young Ellen Gilchrist with great-grandmother Biggs and brother Dooley
(William Garth Gilchrist III)

Paternal grandmother,
Louise Winchester Clark
Gilchrist, of Rosedale,
Mississippi, and Natchez

Paternal grandfather,
William Garth Gilchrist,
Senior, of Courtland,
Alabama

Nell Biggs Alford,
maternal grandmother

Stewart Floyd Alford,
maternal grandfather

Maternal grandmother and grandfather, Aunt Margaret on running board.
Great-grandmother holding mother in back seat, and Onnie Maud

POPULARITY CONTEST
FOR THE
1927 OLE MISS

1.—Most Popular Professor *Dr. Hellerton*
2.—Most Popular Girl *"Bodie" Alford*
3.—Most Popular Man *"Shine" Morgan*
4.—Most Intellectual *Mynes McDougal*
5.—Most Original *"Shine" Morgan*
6.—Most Attractive Girl *Jessie Lea*
7.—Best Dressed Boy *Vencial Greene*
8.—Most Stylish Co-Ed *Charlene Anderson*
9.—Handsomest Man *Fred Bradshaw*
10.—The Wittiest *"Shine" Morgan*
11.—Best-All-Round *Webb Burke*

12.—Who do you think has done more for Ole Miss? Upheld the traditions and standards of Ole Miss most worthly? Given to the school for the student body the best service? Having thought of these, vote for the

Man Who Has Meant Most to Ole Miss
Mynes McDougal

BUY YOUR COPY OF THE '27 OLE MISS NOW!

Ellen Gilchrist's mother, "Bodie"
Alford, listed as "Most Popular Girl,"
Ole Miss, 1927

Mother at Hopedale
with Jiggs and Maggie

Mother at Ole Miss,
1928

54

Ellen Gilchrist's father,
pro-baseball infielder Garth
Gilchrist, known as "Dooley"

Father in 1979

Eli Nailor, baby Ellen, and dogs Old Joe and Bud

Ellen, Stewart Floyd Alford, Senior, her grandfather, and Jiggs

Dooley Gilchrist,
Roosevelt and Henrietta
Neal, and Ellen Gilchrist
on Steele's Bayou, fall of
1936 or 1937

Little Dooley, Eli Nailor,
little Ellen, 1936

Ellen, brother Dooley

Eli Nailor holding
Dooley, George Healy
IV (Bunky), Grand-
father Alford, Roberta
Alford, Roosevelt Neal,
and Old Joe the dog

Jeanne Finney and
Ellen (on right), 1939

Henrietta Neal, Nancy Crane, Ellen, Eli Nailor

Fourth of July parade, about eleven in the morning, Mound City,
Illinois, 1939

INFLUENCES

I AM READING the correspondence of Gustave Flaubert and George Sand. I love these letters. They are a perfect match for me at this time in my life. George Sand was a settled grandmother of fifty-seven when she began this correspondence with a despairing Flaubert. She had given up her wild life and gone to live among her family in the French countryside near Nohant. She had a little granddaughter named Aurore whom she adored and she was deeply involved in the lives of her family and friends. She wrote movingly to Flaubert of their illnesses during the long French winters. There is a great charm about these letters. "A hundred times in life," she declares in one letter, "the good that one does seems to serve no immediate purpose: yet it maintains in one way or another the tradition of well wishing and well doing without which all would perish."

I was thinking of that this morning. I was out walking in my new neighborhood watching the early morning mist rising from these streets that were pasturelands when I left Jackson, Mississippi, eighteen years ago. Well wishing and well doing. How often I have tried to tell writing students that the first thing a writer must do is love the reader and wish the reader well. The writer must trust the reader to be at least as intelligent as he is. Only in such well wishing and trust, only when the writer feels he is writing a letter to a good friend, only then will the magic happen.

I have done the other thing. I have written bitter and cruel things and even published some of them and I regret them every one. This big brain of ours can think of anything. The job of the civilized man or woman is to choose what to keep and what to throw away. I want to love the world as George Sand did. I don't want the bitterness and despair of Flaubert.

His letters to her are full of sadness. He thinks the world is full of stupidity and cruelty and evil. George Sand also saw the evil of the world, but she did not think it was the ground of being. In a radiant passage she defends her utopian political ideals. "Everyone must be happy so that the happiness of a few will not be criminal or cursed by God."

Over and over in these letters Flaubert despairs, George Sand cheers him up and insists he must love the world. Their letters often cross in the mail.

I am sleeping well with this book by my side, feeling privileged to be allowed to share the record of this amazing friendship. The edition I am reading is the translation by Aimee McKenzie and it's hard to find. You will have to go to a library or have the book ordered by a bookstore. Most of the best reading in the world must be searched for in card catalogs or on dusty shelves in the back of stores.

♄

"A BODY does not experience itself as falling through space." Einstein called that the happiest thought of his life. It was the basis of the special theory of relativity and his search for a unified field theory.

A body does not experience itself as falling through space. This does not mean you or me falling from a ladder or the top of a ten-story building, although it can mean that too. It is Monday afternoon. I have been thinking about that concept since Saturday night. I had a debauch Saturday night. You all know what wild lives writers live. It began at four in the afternoon when I made the mistake of going to the bookstore. I left with three books, the New Modern Library edition of *On the Origin of Species* and *The Descent of Man* by Charles

Darwin, a book called *Darwin for Beginners* by Jonathan
Howard, and the Abraham Pais biography of Einstein.

I was excited. I kept stopping on corners and reading. I
went on up the mountain, ran into my house, stuck a diet
dinner in the oven, and settled down on the couch to read.

I opened the Pais book on Einstein and began. "There was
always about him a wonderful purity, at once childlike and
profoundly stubborn. It is no art to be an idealist if one lives
in cloud cuckoo land. He, however, was an idealist even
though he lived on earth and knew its smell better than
almost anyone else.

"Nothing was more alien to Einstein than to settle any
issue by compromise, in his life or in his science. When he
spoke on political problems he always steered toward their
answer. Were I asked for a one-sentence biography of
Einstein I would say he was the freest man I have ever
known."

Oh, my God, I said. This will take the wide net. I turned
off the diet dinner, picked up the phone, ordered a large
combination pizza, and settled down — about nine thirty I
could take no more. I went on off to bed. As always when I
attempt to read about physics I am filled with wonder, a
sense of ecstasy, pattern, texture, design. "Subtle is the
Lord," Einstein said, "but he is not malicious." We are
allowed to see what is going on. I went to bed without
washing my face or hands. I snuggled deep down into the
covers, for it is still winter here. I dreamed of fields of green
going out from me in all directions. I was the center of the
dream but not of the world. I fit into the plan of the world.
I was in the right place and I could move. The fields stretched
out — on and on — there was nothing frightening anywhere.
Nothing that could not be seen and wondered at and
understood. Nowhere I could not go by walking. I was not
hungry or tired or scared. There were no snakes behind me in
the grass, no insurmountable hills to climb, no unbridled
horses coming to ride me down, no cars plummeting down
hills toward water, no dragons to slay.

In the night I woke and opened all the windows so I could hear the wind blowing across the Ozarks. A body does not experience itself as falling through space. Because there is no fall and there is no space.

♈

I WILL BE fifty years old tomorrow. My fiftieth year to heaven, as Dylan Thomas once wrote. I read that very long poem out loud to myself every year on my birthday.

This year I am going to spend my birthday with the work of another genius. I don't know what genius is, but I know that when it breaks forth among us we recognize it and protect and cherish the gifts it leaves us. Bona fide geniuses are almost always very careless about leaving their work around in unprotected places. As if they know someone will take care of it for them. Or, perhaps, they can afford to be careless since they understand it springs from abundance, from an inexhaustible well.

All men honor genius, in all times, in all cultures, because it shows the rest of us what we can be, what we are made of, this dazzling, complicated creature we call man.

For my birthday, I am going to visit a house painted by a genius. The whole interior of the house is a mural of such brilliance and light that there is no way to describe its effect upon the mind of the viewer. Looking at that mural is like watching a child dance or a bird in flight. The mural was painted by Walter Inglis Anderson, who lived and worked in a place called Shearwater Pottery in Ocean Springs, Mississippi. Here, among his family and his children, protected from the world, he painted hundreds and hundreds of brilliant watercolors. He also carved huge wooden sculptures from fallen tree trunks and made murals and woodcuts and pottery and illustrations for children's books.

No one bothered him. No one told him to stop, or to do it another way. So he just got up every morning and did the work of a genius.

Often he threw a gunnysack full of canned goods into the bottom of a rowboat and rowed out into the Gulf of Mexico to a small deserted island that is part of the barrier reef that guards the Mississippi coast. There he painted everything that lives and breathes and moves. Hundreds of perfectly achieved watercolors on one and sometimes two sides of quite ordinary typewriter paper. When Hurricane Camille was on the way, he rowed out to the island and tied himself to a tree to ride out the storm protecting his island from the elements.

Genius is like a wild thumbprint. You can never look at trees or water or animals or yourself in quite the same way again after you have shared his vision. All he saw was magic and yet there is an orderly and logical intelligence to everything he wrote or painted. Pattern, texture, design, weave and weave and weave. "Wing, wind, wave. Wave, wind, wing."

He was in the habit of dashing off notes to himself on scraps of paper. On the backs of drawings or in the logs of his trips to Horn Island. Verses, aphorisms, stories, essays. An overwhelming mass of bits and pieces that fit together to reveal the shape of the quest he was on.

Here are some of the things he had to say.

"It is literally true that the demon to the student is technique. And it really is evil. Pay no attention to it, either in dancing or in painting."

"The evil to the beginning painter is confusion. Too many details. As he learns technique he forgets his demon and thinks he has defeated him with technique, but he has just given him a hiding place."

"True art consists of spreading wide the intervals so that the imagination may fill the spaces between the trees."

"The normal or even fairly normal man has to be almost knocked down physically to be anything but sublime. Why this is done I don't know. What reason is there against man realizing his sublimity I don't know."

"It is strange that the artist should have no standards and be constantly trying to live up to other people's standards."

"This is the supposition. I live and have my being in a world of space and forms which have color and shape. Consciousness of this means being alive."

"The first poetry is always written against the wind by sailors and farmers who sing with the wind in their teeth. The second poetry is written by scholars and wine drinkers who know a good thing when they see it. The third poetry is sometimes never written but when it is, it's by those who have brought nature and art together into one thing."

Tomorrow I will visit the house where the genius Walter Anderson slept while he was among us. As he wrote:

"If my ears were functioning properly I would hear, not just the wind in the grass, the two or three different rhythms of insects, the piping of a frog, the call of a nightjar, but an orderly and recognizable harmony, which might or might not have been written."

"A divine symphony. Wind, wave, wing . . . wing, wave, wind."

THIS IS part of a speech I wrote to celebrate Founder's Day at Scripps College in Claremont, California. I liked writing this speech because it gave me a chance to talk about something that is much on my mind right now. How wonderful men and women are and how long we have been wonderful. I wrote the speech four times. It ended up being more like a play in four acts than a speech. Here is Act Four.

I want to leave you with the idea that no theory is too wild to entertain for a while. You can entertain all the ideas you can think up or imagine. Later, in winter, you can decide which ones to keep and which to throw away. All of us are doing the same thing all the time anyway, all probing the same mystery, asking the same questions. Who am I? Where did I come from? What am I doing here? Is this right?

At the moment I have decided that for all practical purposes I can go on and assume that mankind, our species, *Homo sapiens sapiens,* is the only thing in the universe that is aware of itself. Our species, Man, on this beautiful watery planet, in this little piece of space and time, may be the only thing in the universe that ever was or ever will be aware of itself.

I have been reading a book by the scientist and philosopher René Dubos, called *Celebrations of Life.* Dr. Dubos writes about Neanderthal man, who was here on the earth one hundred thousand years ago. It used to be thought that these people were brutish and primitive, but they walked erect just like us and had brains as large or maybe larger. They had a full kit of tools, and, strangest of all, every fifth person in their bands has been identified as being over fifty years of age. This is amazing for a primitive hunting society.

Two of the old Neanderthal people found in the caves at Shandar in Iraq were so severely crippled that they must have been completely dependent on the members of their group for a long time. Also, these people buried their dead in graves lined with flowers. Clearly, we have been human for a long time. Clearly the first thing we did was probe the mystery and the last thing we will ever do is probe that same mystery.

INFLUENCES

℞

I TAUGHT MYSELF to read poetry. Long before I could read prose
I could piece together the words of nursery rhymes and
poems. Long before I went to school I knew passages of
Wordsworth by heart and the lyrics of many songs and would
make up my own and write them down.

> *I am very happy now*
> *Dooley is dead and in his grave*
> *All his stuff belongs to me*
> *It's not my fault he drank poison tea*

Sometimes I would leave sibling rivalry as a subject for
verse and branch out into metaphysics.

> *Oh, I love rain so much*
> *I love the skies and everything God made*
> *I hope he likes me too. If he doesn't, too bad for him*

I was mad at God. He had created a world full of bugs to
bite me. Why did he make them? It made no sense to me.
Later, when I was really angry with him about death, I
thought back on his invention of bugs and knew that I had
every right to be furious. If God made the world he wasn't
good enough for me.

I think I knew early on that poets were as angry with God
as I was. Certainly they were angry about death. Humpty
Dumpty, what cynicism, what irony. All the King's horses
and all the King's men. Thee and thou, the language of the
Bible. A lot of sound and fury to cover up what God had done
to us. I hated him. I sat up in a magnolia tree getting black
from the bark and dared him to make me fall. I threw myself
into rivers and dared him to make me forget how to swim. I
filled my mouth with water and spat at the sun. Nothing

happened. If he existed he was powerless. God reminded me too much of my father to be in good with me.

So poetry took the place of God. The wild cries of a thousand minds saying, Why did you do this, God? Who are you and why have you done this and since you did it, at least I'm going to call you on it. At least I'm going to make you stand up and face what you have done. My Last Duchess, the sphinx in the desert, oh, what are patterns for, Not one deserted dying, on whose forbidden ear, Go, Go, Go, human kind cannot bear very much reality.

On and on and on. Of course, there were also cries of lyricism and of love. I wandered lonely as a cloud, All I could see from where I stood, Oh, world, world, I cannot hold thee close enough. I also emitted great cries of praise, but not of God. It was man I was praising and the beauty of the earth.

Later, thinking over that poem about daffodils, I decided the main word in the poem was *lonely*. God makes us lonely and makes us die and the earth consoles us and gives suck, gives beauty beyond description and we go on another day.

How could men go into churches and praise the thing they call God? I asked myself. How could they praise something that has control over them, that rules them. What a bunch of bullshit. That's a poetic word I learned that came in handy when I was forced to sit in starched dresses and listen to preachers droning on in their sonorous and boring voices with that glazed look that comes over the faces of panderers and inveterate liars. I would squirm around on the seat. I would count the number of letters in the program, not counting punctuation marks; if the sum was an odd number, it meant Dick Lockwood loved me. If it was an even number, he did not. If it was an even number, I would do a recount including the punctuation marks. If it still came out even, I tore the program up and counted the words in a hymn.

That's what came next: after the panderer had put us all to sleep he would bring out a piece of music written by Bach and give God credit for that. The service would brighten up with the first chord of music from the organ. We would lift up our eyes unto the hills where the real world would hopefully still be going on when we got out of church. What was that all about? A poet knew.

ah Galexea Galexea
to think it was your own little whim
to invent him this man
What was it?
that you couldn't look with your own eyes
at your armpit?
you couldn't see your own beautiful back
graceful as a beach
and you wanted someone to walk
its lovely loneliness a while?
a while only?

That is part of a long poem by Alvaro Cordona-Hine, and I have kept it with me for years and read it to thousands of people and once read it on National Public Radio and once read it late at night to a room full of people at a Book and Author dinner who probably had something else in mind besides hearing me read a long philosophical poem by a real writer. I read the poem and then I got up and left so I wouldn't have to hear the speeches made by the romance novel writer and the country-and-western writer wearing the hat and smoking the big cigar while we ate dinner. After that night my publisher decided it would be best to keep me home and sell the books the best they could without me.

But I was talking about poetry. There weren't any poets at the Book and Author dinner. There aren't many poets anywhere anymore because the poetry isn't lyrical or much good or memorable and besides no one wants to read it but the same bunch of teacher-poets who write it and they are too cornered to allow anything wonderful to happen in poetry. If a good poet begins to raise his or her voice, they kill him with criticism. "Lyrical wheel-spinning," that's the kind of thing they say to young poets who are letting their hearts sing. So no one loves poetry anymore and no one wants to publish it and no one wants to buy it and all of that has taken the heart out of young poets. If a young poet showed up today with a poem that began, "It was my thirtieth year to heaven," he would be laughed off the block.

Here are some of the poets it is no longer fashionable to emulate. Edna St. Vincent Millay, who at nineteen could write, "All I could see from where I stood / Was three long mountains and a wood; / I turned and looked another way, / And saw three islands in a bay. . . . Over these things I could not see; / These were the things that bounded me."

Anne Sexton is another poet the Academy would like to forget if possible or at least send to the back of the class. Anthologies never do her work justice and she is being passed over as a subject for serious study. Still, while she was writing she spoke to us with a voice as real and lyrical as the sea and my generation of women learned about ourselves from her. "I am torn in two but I will conquer myself," she wrote. "I will take scissors and cut out the beggar. I will take a crowbar and pry out the broken pieces of God in me."

"The sea is very old," she wrote. "The sea is the face of Mary, / without miracles or rage / or unusual hope." And

I am surprised to see
that the ocean is still going on.
Now I am going back
and I have ripped my hand
from your hand as I said I would
and I have made it this far
as I said I would
and I am on the top deck now
holding my wallet, my cigarettes
and my car keys
at 2 o'clock on a Tuesday
in August of 1960.

How I love the wild lyrical language of the poets. I knew a poet once and spent many days and nights with him and took walks with him and went into shops with him and watched the world with him and learned to adore the beauty of the world and despise its sadness. I must write of him someday and tell the world what it was like to know a great poet and be his friend. When he killed himself over some long-buried sadness, I could not bear to remember him and threw away all his books and all his letters and everything that had anything to do with him except an unpublished manuscript that was dedicated to me. It's still around. Even in my sadness and rage I couldn't throw that away.

What else? The Arabs believe there are three causes for celebration. The birth of a son, the foaling of a stallion, and the emergence of a poet. One is emerging somewhere now who will write the poem that will solace and teach me in my old age. I raise a glass to that poet and dedicate my song to him.

CP

FIFTEEN YEARS AGO I bought my first real painting. I remember the strange quality of that week, while the painting sat in my living room, and while I pondered the possibility of actually spending *three hundred and fifty dollars* for something to hang on a wall.

On the side of buying the painting was a line I had read somewhere by Gertrude Stein. She had said you can either have great paintings or you can have great clothes, and that she had chosen to have paintings. Also, I kept remembering once when I was nineteen years old and was in Birmingham, Alabama, with fifty dollars to spend. It was a bright January day at the end of Christmas vacation and I was standing on a sidewalk halfway in between a clothing store, where a pair of gold cocktail shoes with three-inch heels was begging me to buy them, and an antique store, where an old handmade cobbler's bench was on sale for exactly the cost of the shoes. I kept going back into the antique store and marveling at the patina on the wood of the bench, sitting on it, as a real cobbler once sat, and rubbing my hands along the smooth dark sides.

In the end I went into the clothing store and bought the tight uncomfortable golden shoes and left the bench. I had cast my lot with vanity and I knew it. That bench haunted me for years. Every time I wanted a table to go beside a sofa or a place for a child to sit and color I would think about the wide purpose of the bench, the intelligence of its design.

Meanwhile the golden shoes had carried me to a lot of drunken fraternity parties and disappeared into the destiny of cocktail clothes.

Now, some years later, I walked in and out of my living room past the beautiful painting that I was trying to make up my mind to buy. It was the first work I had seen by the American realist Ginny Crouch Stanford, who later would become my friend and paint the brilliant paintings which would become my book covers, and the story of that damn cobbler's bench kept pounding in my head, a moral tale if there ever was one.

Finally I gave in. I wrote a check and mailed it off and the painting was mine. I think I should note that I was properly appalled that I could so easily become the proprietor of another person's work and ran out and wrote a will leaving the painting to the painter at my death.

It is still my favorite painting. It keeps getting closer to me. It hung for many years above a fireplace. Then above a baby grand piano. Now it is beside my bed, on a wall that looks out upon a lake. "Those eyes," people say when they look at it, meaning the beautiful, haunting face of the young black-haired girl who leans in the painting against a marble statue of an angel. "My God, those eyes."

"I know," I answer. How long that painted look has lasted and never lost its power to charm and amaze.

Once I made that initial plunge into buying art, the rest was easy. I didn't buy another pair of high-heeled shoes for years. I didn't buy cocktail clothes or new placemats or recover the sofa. My money was spent on paintings and pieces of sculpture and pottery and photographs. By the time I left New Orleans and went to live in a simple light-filled house in the Ozark Mountains, the only things I cared enough about to pack up and take with me were these beautiful individual products of other minds and hands. For seven years I lived alone in a small frame house on a mountain and hardly ever bothered to lock the door. Anybody that wanted to steal the things in that house would have been someone I wanted to meet. I don't think I ever lost sight of how fortunate I was to spend my days and nights surrounded by the best moments of some of the best minds of my culture.

Finally, I had accumulated too much wonder. I was in danger of becoming a museum curator, which is a fine occupation but not a good thing for a writer, who needs to travel light and stay flexible.

So I have gone into phase two of my fascination with art. I have started giving it away. I am fortunate in having three sons who also love beautiful things, and among them I am able to keep many walls and flat surfaces covered with art in various cities in the southeastern part of the United States. I lend them paintings and photographs and they lend them back to me. I will turn a corner in one of my children's houses and there is a painting I bought one snowy January day in Boulder, Colorado, or, I'll enter a room in an apartment and there is a piece of pottery from the day I discovered the famous Calabash potters of Fayetteville, Arkansas.

Life will not give us everything we want. It will not give us happiness, or "the seven Visigoth crowns in the Cluny Museum," as Elinor Wylie once wrote. But it may give us "a very small purse, made of a mouse's hide. Put it in your pocket and never look inside."

Art civilizes and makes clear. Living with art is charming, in the old sense of the word. The art object draws you into it, does a little dance for you, calls up, praises, sings. God Love Artists, my daughter-in-law once wrote to me on a postcard from the Museum of Modern Art's exhibit of Picasso. They Make It Right.

♈

THE NEW ORLEANS PHOTOGRAPHER Clarence Laughlin was a friend of mine. He was a genius. Genius can not be dissected or understood. It can only be loved and celebrated and wondered at.

Clarence was a New Orleanian and proud of that fact, but in his heart I think he was always a child of the bayou country. He drank its sugary wines and honored its legends until his death this January at eighty. He gave up its sugary tongue, however, and taught himself to speak in such a way that almost no trace of his Cajun accent remained. More about this later. First I want to talk about his magic.

Everything about Clarence was magical. In his presence you could believe in magic or destiny or kismet. He thought it was kismet that we came to know each other. He felt this way about many of his friends.

I had heard of Clarence. One day another photographer came tearing into the offices of *The Courier,* where we both worked, showing us photographs and copy for a story about Clarence. "You won't believe this man," he was saying, or words to that effect. "He's incredible. He knows everything." I looked at the photographs. There was this smooth-cheeked white-haired man with piercing eyes already demanding something from me. Some answer. Some return. There were also pages of quotations. I read them with great interest and attention.

About a month later a friend took me, on a cold rainy Sunday afternoon, down to the Faubourg-Marigny to see an exhibition of Clarence's work and hear him speak. It was a new gallery with tall freshly painted walls and high ceilings. People were milling around drinking wine and talking in quiet voices. There was violin music on the stereo. And on the walls were the most incredible photographs I had ever seen. Absolutely original, as was their maker. He came into the gallery, wearing a coat thrown over his shoulder like a cape, and took the podium and began to talk about art in a way I had never heard. About the relationship between art and the subconscious mind, about the forms art takes in its insistence on telling us what we're thinking. About how art takes us past the veils of illusion and returns us to ourselves. About what a photograph means and why light and shadow fascinate us, about how unique we are and how alike, how mysterious we are and how predictable. I was dazzled.

I ordered two photographs and went home and wrote him a long letter in answer to the questions he had raised in my mind. Later, when I knew Clarence well and became his friend, I would drive him to the Lafayette Station post office to pick up his mail, boxes of fan mail from all over the world. I suppose when I wrote him I thought I was the only one who did.

Anyway, I mailed off the letter, not expecting or even particularly wanting a reply, and in a few days he called me. There was his rough, exciting, enormously civilized voice on the phone, inviting me down to the Pontalba to see his books.

At that time he had a huge apartment in the Pontalba overlooking Jackson Square. It contained a library of almost two hundred thousand volumes. They were the most incredible books I had ever seen. Clarence slept on a small bed in the midst of those bookshelves. He could put his finger on any book without consulting a catalog. But then, he only got out the ones he was interested in. You could ask all night but he would not produce a book he didn't want to talk about.

As soon as I arrived that first night we went right to work. Clarence got out some books and began my education. "Look," he would say, "look at this. You must understand this. Listen to what I'm telling you." Leonor Fini, the French surrealist poets, Balthus, Klimt, Lafcadio Hearn, British illustrators, Italian cartoonists, the lists of things I must learn and "be exposed to" went on and on.

Oil interests in the gulf, people destroying the wetlands, plastic cups, undisciplined children, women smokers, unlettered so-called writers, Mayor Moon's attempts to bring a sound and light show into Jackson Square, the list of things he hated and warred against was also long.

"But, Clarence," I would say finally, "I want to see your photographs. I came to see your photographs. Please show them to me." Then, grumbling, he would get out a stack of prints and begin to tell me how they were created. Created they were. Planned and executed with the care an architect takes with a building. Only Clarence was the planner *and* the builder *and* the carpenter and the plumber and the one that cut the trees down to get the lumber.

It wasn't easy being his friend. You had to be able to move fast. Clarence was full of ideas and he feared nothing except having his knee give out or his books cut up by greedy dealers. He was haunted by the idea that someone would get hold of his treasured art books and cut them up and sell the pages.

At the height of my friendship with Clarence he had me in a car one spring day driving down to Terrebone Parish with four surrealists from Chicago in the back seat. We were going to see the cemeteries. I was driving my small blue Datsun. The surrealists were huddled together in the back seat. Clarence was riding shotgun, telling me how to drive and reading the map and lecturing about Cajun cults of death and black silk funeral flowers and enamel photographs of the dead and carvings on tombstones and surrealism in general and the bad state of the arts.

He turned to me suddenly, as if he had just remembered something important. "I've been meaning to tell you that whenever you have time we can start our diction lessons," he said.

"What?" I answered, for this was new to me.

"I've decided to teach you to speak properly," he said. "So that people will take you seriously." The surrealists looked down at their hands, embarrassed for me.

"That's okay," I said. "I'll just stay like I am."

"Of course not," he said, and went back to the map. "It took me a long time to learn to speak correctly but I learned. You will learn too." Alas, we never had time for our lessons.

I learned of his death by reading of it in *Time* magazine. It was a cold wet winter evening. I was at a newsstand on the corner of Third Avenue and 73rd Street in New York City. I bought the magazine and stuck it in my pocket and walked outside and stood on the street thinking about the last time I had seen him, the night he showed me his new darkroom in the library he built onto the back of his wife Elizabeth's house in Gentilly. Then I thought about the last month he spent in the Pontalba, about how bad his knee had become and how he cursed it. About the hundreds of boxes of books he had packed and the pulley system and cardboard chute he invented to lower the boxes down the three flights of narrow rickety Pontalba stairs. I thought about the expression on our faces as Clarence outlined his plan to sail the boxes down from floor to floor.

That night I had a dream. In the morning I began to develop it into one of my Journal Entries for National Public Radio. The dream appeared to be about Picasso but as I developed it I saw it was really about Clarence. In such a way the mind gives up its secrets. I call it magic. Clarence called it art. Here then is the dream and its unfolding.

Journal entry, January 18, 1985,
New York City, New York

I dreamed last night of Picasso. We were driving through the Delta looking for a house for him to use as a studio. We were in my little blue Toyota. I was driving. Picasso was in the jump seat. "They gave me everything I wanted," Picasso said. "Money and fame and beautiful lovers."

"They let you paint your chairs," I said. "That was the good part."

"I painted what they wanted," he said. "The more ridiculous it was the more they liked it."

"You were a genius at fourteen," I said. "What else could you do? You had to find ways to make it more amusing."

"I needed blue," he said. "I wanted a blue made of ground-up sapphires. If I had had the right blue. It really made me mad not to find that blue."

"You did all right," I said. "You did just fine."

"Guernica," he said. "They all wanted *Guernica.* Look at the drawings, I told them. Look at the eyes on the women. Look at the love scenes. *Guernica,* they demanded. Show us war."

"It was wild," I said and we laughed together at that. Two artists out for a drive in the country. It was a bright spring day in the Delta. The sun made mirages on the asphalt road.

"I was always afraid of running out of water in the desert," Picasso said. "I was afraid I would end up chasing mirages."

"That's deep," I said. "That's very deep."

"I know," he said and settled down into the jump seat. "But who can bear to live on the surface?"

In real life I also hang out with painters and potters and photographers. They are the best friends a writer has. They teach you to use your eyes.

Clarence Laughlin was my first artist friend after I started writing, a wonderful, outlandish, completely original man. He gave me the cover for my first book of poems. Just gave it to me. A beautiful photograph of a Welsh actress. One night Clarence came to my house to take me to a double feature art film. *Siddhartha* and *Steppenwolf*. My husband came home as Clarence and I were leaving and asked politely if I would make him a sandwich before I left. Clarence hit the ceiling. We are going to see art, he said, drawing himself up on his walking stick. You can eat anytime.

My husband apologized, grabbed a piece of cold bread, and the three of us rushed off to the movies.

I WAS OUT WALKING on the mountain with a friend named Kathy last week. She had just returned from a visit to Seattle, and was full of descriptions of the mountains and the forests and the wildflowers. She told me she had run into an old friend named Greg who said he was driving to work one day last February and heard me say on the radio that we should all learn from two-year-olds and go to work by different routes and take all our books off the shelves and throw them on the floor and play with them.

So that afternoon he went out and bought a red motorcycle and named it for me and now he goes to work in a different way.

"Oh, no," I said to Kathy. "I'm scared to death of motorcycles."

"Don't worry," she said. "He's a responsible person. He'll be careful and not get hurt."

It was the first cool day. We walked awhile in silence. I kept thinking about all the ruts I've let myself get into lately and how I can talk a good game but where is the action and so forth. Kathy turned off on Spring Street and I walked on home and went into my house and started pulling all the books off my bookshelves and piling them up on the living-room floor. Pretty soon I had a carpet of books. It looked great. I found a set of charcoals behind the books and drew a picture of myself and then one of a tree and then I found an old Japanese fan I bought years ago in New Orleans. Then I sat down to read. I found Loren Eiseley's *The Star Thrower* and my book of Karsh's photographs and I marveled over the photographs of Tennessee Williams and the mystical one of Martin Luther King.

I am here to report that my advice about taking down those books was sound. Not only was it a good idea but it was the beginning of one of the best weekends I've ever had. I picked up Judy Dater's book of photographs with the wonderful cover photograph of Imogen Cunningham standing by a tree in her long black dress with her camera strap embroidered with peace signs and went downtown to show it to someone. I wandered into the Restaurant on the Corner and found the jazz pianist, Leland Tamboulian, and he wanted to see the books so he came up and played the piano while the sun went down and some more people came over and someone found *The Rubáiyát* of Omar Khayyám and had to read it out loud and one thing led to another and the whole weekend was infused with a wonderful sense of fun and good humor all thanks to Greg Simon of Seattle, Washington, who reminded me of something I must have known for a while in February but had forgotten in the dog days of August.

WORK

$\mathcal{H}$OLLYWOOD AND the writer: so the first thing that happened was I had this successful book of short stories called *In the Land of Dreamy Dreams*. That same year the twenty-five-year-old daughter of a friend in Jackson, Mississippi, won a Pulitzer Prize for a play. She was out in Hollywood turning down offers as fast as she could answer the phone, so she told one of the producers at Twentieth Century Fox to call and offer one of the deals to me. Deals, that's what they call them out there. It reminds me of my brother and me matching nickels with our lunch money in the sixth grade.

I was in my kitchen in Fayetteville, Arkansas, one afternoon in 1980 and the phone rang. It was a businesslike voice calling from Hollywood and offering to give me sixty-five thousand dollars to rewrite the Italian film *Wife-mistress* and set it in New Orleans. You've got to be kidding, I said. Why on earth would you want to do something like that?

That was before I knew you are supposed to say, Oh, yes, what a marvelous idea. How did you ever think up something so wonderful? That is the proper response to a Hollywood producer. Oh, my, what a wonderful brilliant idea. Gee, I'm honored you called me in on that. Besides, I didn't know anything about publishing or movies at the time and I thought sixty-five thousand dollars must be some magic number of dollars they gave away right and left. I had just been offered almost exactly that amount of money for something else someone thought up for me to do. I didn't know yet that all you got to begin with — up front, they call it — was a very small amount of money and you had to work for months or years even and then it was highly unlikely that they would ever give you the rest of the money. Also they make you feel like it's you who has failed, never that it was they that couldn't pull the deal off — Hollywood is really as sleazy as it's reported to be. It chews up writers and spits them out. It wastes their time and their dreams.

I didn't know any of this yet. "Well, listen," I told this producer, trying to make her feel better about coming up with such a dumb idea, "I've got a lot better ideas than that for making movies." Oh, she said, tell me. So I told her the entire plots of about three movies and even called her back on my own money to finish one I had to interrupt to go to the door. So she wrote that all down and I never heard from her again.

I found all of that very interesting. Later I had some more offers of about the same kind — I just kept turning them down. I am saving myself for something I can believe in — that's how crazy I am.

༆

UNIVERSITIES are always after me to give them my papers (by which they mean my letters and notes and worksheets). Whenever that happens I go out to the shed and get a sack of them and burn them up in the wood stove. I hate the idea of some poor graduate student down in a marble basement somewhere going through my notes and letters and wild imaginings. These pieces of paper are meaningful to me because any time I look at one of them it reminds me of what I was doing when I wrote it. But why should some stranger waste his time on my worksheets?

A poet told me a good one the other day. She said academics have a new name for a writer's worksheets. They call them repressed papers. Here are some of my repressed papers. I found this notebook on the floor by the piano this morning. It's been there for months.

To comprehend the major blueprints. An event occurs in three dimensions of space and one of time, or motion?

A four dimensional space time continuum. Is time motion? Yes, it seems so.
The simpler the premises the wider the area of applicability.
The heuristic view that light can be both wave and particle.
The questioning of causality. Always we have taken for granted the idea that every event could be explained by its antecedent conditions.

What is random?
DO THE LAWS OF CAUSE AND EFFECT GIVE WAY TO THE LAWS OF CHANCE AT THE ATOMIC LEVEL?
The equivalence of all inertial systems in regard to light.
Inertia. The tendency of a body to resist acceleration.
Light is composed of discrete packets or quanta which move without subdividing and which are absorbed and emitted only as units.
Light is composed of quanta.
The study of the very small is quantum physics and the study of the vast realms of space is relativity.

I will name the new book *Light Can Be Both Wave and Particle*. In memory of *Everything That Rises Must Converge*. Remember how that title haunted me and how hard I tried to know what it meant? Yes, *Light Can Be Both Wave and Particle*.

WORK

* * *

"Wave and particle?" my editor said and shook his head.
"Why not, it suits me if it suits you."

♀

MORE REPRESSED PAPERS:

I would still be a writer whether or not I had ever been
in psychoanalysis but I would be a different writer,
more driven, frightened, wild and unsure, a poet hiding
behind the mask of poetry, talking in riddles,
obsessed for days with words like riddles,
caught in traps of language,
unable to understand the sources of language or my own
subconscious motivations and drives.
I would not know as much, maybe.
Maybe I found out as much writing as I did talking.

Psychoanalysis is the impossible profession. The terrible
paradox is that the knowledge gained by psychoanalysis is not
of much use in the real world. No, that's not true. It's of use
to a writer. The terrible problem is that the knowledge is not
transferable.

My Freudian said I was not in analysis. I would never lie
down on the couch. I sat cross-legged on the floor looking at
his shoes. He would never let me touch his shoes. Anyway,
I think I am funnier and wiser and more balanced because of
it. I like myself more and trust myself more. Of course, I
might have been that way because I got older. Or maybe it's

just because I've gotten up every day for eight years and done my work and am still doing it. Maybe my work healed me of the small amount of civilizing I was exposed to. Guilt is too high a price to pay for civilization. There's got to be a better way.

I was sitting on a bed in a New York apartment arguing with my cousin about God.

"Who made you?" she demanded.

"I don't know."

"You think you're so powerful you made yourself?"

"I didn't say that, Baby Gwen, you said that, don't put words in my mouth."

"Then what do you believe? Even you have to believe in something."

"I believe that man takes his own goodness and sets that intelligence outside of himself and calls it God and worships it. And then he takes his natural ability to transmit thoughts and he calls that the power of prayer. It's all semantics. It's all words."

"You have to make the leap of faith. Someday you'll do it."

"I will not."

"It's all faith. It's faith and grace."

"It's twelve o'clock, Baby Gwen, and we've been arguing this for thirty-seven years. I'm going home."

We get up from our mutual great-great-grandfather's bed which my cousin keeps in an apartment in New York. We hug and kiss and go our separate ways.

I walk out into the streets of New York City at night. Lights that man invented and made out of his greatness are all.over the place on the streets and above. Through a crack in the skyscrapers are other lights, wildly, crazily dependable somehow or other in case it is true that the earth is round and moving on its axis among the stars.

☿

I KNOW a lot of two-year-olds that have genius. They are terribly observant, absolutely curious, willing to take risks. They will pay endless attention to detail, will return over and over again to a problem until it's solved. Suddenly, they make the final move, the cap is off the bottle, the cabinet is open, the door is unlatched. My children were escape artists. They ran away to have adventures. I have chased them through the streets a million times, in my nightgown or in the rain. The oldest one was the best at it. When I found him he would be sitting in some stranger's house eating cookies. He knew how to pick his victims. They would usually be people about the age I am now. Do you remember how marvelous a stranger's house smelled when you were small? That's another mark of genius, the senses are keen and finely tuned.

How to hold on to that native genius and also learn the things we need to know to survive. How to hold on to the breadth of genius and still narrow it down enough to concentrate on one piece of work. How not to allow the narrowing to become more important than the whole. These are big problems. I'm thinking about them all the time. How not to let the world de-genius us, our children and our grandchildren and our friends.

Here's one thing I know for sure — you have to stay flexible. You have to have a lot of possible moves so no one can get you in a position where you think there's only one way to live or only one way to solve a problem. A Jungian I know used to make me so mad telling me a story over and over about a friend of his who refuses to eat in the same restaurant twice or drive the same route to work in the morning. Oh, I know, I would say when he told me that story. You've already told me that, don't tell me that again.

No, he would answer, hear me, you aren't listening. Then he would tell it to me again. It was a long time before I began to see the wisdom of that story. Every time I would do something like take a different path when I walked downtown, I would say, Oh, my God, this is so silly.

It is silly. That's the point. It's divine and silly. It's the stuff that genius lives on. To constantly sample the riches and variety of life. Watch a child move from one activity to the other, moving around a house, never exhausting the possibilities of any one thing before moving on to the next one. We say of children, they are into everything. We should be into everything. We should get up one morning and take all our books and put them in a pile in the middle of the floor and start playing with them. Euripides and Aeschylus and Hemingway and Thornton Wilder and Margaret Mead. Faulkner and Edna Millay, and oh, yes, *The Conquest of Mexico* and *The Conquest of Peru* which I borrowed years ago from my ex-husband. Maybe I'll mail them back to him for his birthday.

℞

I AM GEARING UP to go to New York for two weeks to oversee a professional reading of my play. It is a play that I began in New York in February of 1984. I began writing it during the first act of Sam Shepard's *Fool for Love.* I wrote all over my program and my agent's program. Then I went home through a blinding New York rainstorm and wrote all night in a hotel room. The next day I had lunch with my agent and told him I'd been up all night writing a play.

I told him the story, then I put the play away for three months. In June I had to go to Lincoln, Nebraska, to teach for a few weeks so I took the notes with me and there, in a basement apartment near the campus, I hammered out three full acts in less than a week and sent it to a typist.

Since that time the play has undergone four major revisions, elaborating and extending what is there, taking stuff out of the stage directions, which at one time contained a lot of the best material, and putting it back into the play. I am, after all, a fiction writer not a playwright and had to transpose the work from one form to the other.

Now, the American Place Theatre is going to have a professional reading of the play with a fine actress playing the lead. I'm excited and scared, but the day I no longer do anything that frightens me and makes me shy I will know I am finished as a writer. And of course I'm hoping that around eleven o'clock one night they will say, "Oh, Ellen, you have to rewrite the second act," and I'll say, "Don't worry, I'll do it tonight," and so forth. I'll emerge from a hotel room the next morning holding a brilliant revision and everyone will cheer. I keep thinking about a passage from a book by Georges Simenon.

"Why do we read?" he asks, "why do we go to a show? Imagine an entomologist, an observer of insect life, suddenly witnessing the exodus of a quarter of the inhabitants of an anthill, at a time of day when they normally would be sleeping. They are going off to a mysterious appointment. He sees them jostling each other and converging towards a clearing where the soil rises in tiers. In order to enter that enclosure each ant must surrender part of his winter provisions to a sharp-eyed official.

"Why have they left the shelter of the anthill and undertaken this long march? What are they waiting for, motionless and quivering with their gazes turned to a small circle of earth?

"Imagine the shock to our entomologist if he saw five or

ten ants, no different in any way from the others, move forward into the light and amidst an almost religious silence, begin to mime a scene from the life of the ants."

$$\text{우}$$

A FRIEND of mine had dinner with the president of a large makeup company the other day. It's all fear, the president told him. That's our key word. Keep them afraid that no one will love them and you can sell them anything.

I have pondered this little story. Several years ago I became angry at a friend for questioning a column I wrote for *Southern Living* magazine. "Puss," he said, "what's going on? What's happened to you?" "Nothing," I replied, getting really mad at him. "It's just a magazine article, that's all."

The article was about how I'd gone down to Jackson, Mississippi, to visit my mother and as soon as I got off the airplane she told me I looked like Daisy Mae. I was wearing a short denim skirt and leather sandals and a cotton shirt tied around my waist. Actually, I looked just fine. My hair was long and loose, my skin was clear and the color it turns all by itself in the sun. I looked about as good as I can look.

By week's end I was a different person. Jackson, Mississippi, had done a number on me. I had reverted to type, turned myself back into a frightened sorority girl. I had bought a lot of useless clothes and spent two hundred dollars on makeup and ruined my hair with a permanent.

The magazine article I wrote about all that left the reader with the impression that I thought it was very funny. A lipstick costs eight dollars this year. You have to do a lot of

work that someone else thinks up for you to afford that kind
of fear.

ᴄᴘ

Sᴜᴍᴍᴇʀ ɪs ᴛʜᴇ ᴛɪᴍᴇ to deal with paradoxes, with questions
that have no answers, problems that can only be surrounded,
laid siege to. The Castle of Fat is such a problem. The Castle
of Fat is surrounded by a moat of self-deception and
absurdities. High walls of fantasy surround it. Evil guards of
self-hate man the towers. In the square is an everlasting
spring of Diet Coke from which the inhabitants draw
sustenance.

Some of my friends and I have set out to besiege the castle.
First of all we have to decide whether we are fat or not. I was
in conference one afternoon recently with a philosopher and a
retired United Airlines pilot. We had been for a long walk
around the mountain. Afterwards, we were in the philosopher's kitchen and we were talking about fat.
"I don't know if I'm fat or not," I said. "That's what
plagues me. I might not even be fat. I might just think
I'm fat."
"The brain has to have glucose," the pilot said. "That's a
fact."
"The part I hate," the philosopher said, "the part I cannot
deal with, is that a grown man would take off his underpants
to weigh himself."
"Correct," the pilot agreed. We sank our chins deep into
our hands to think it over.
"Why do you think you're fat?" the pilot asked.
"Because I can't button my skirts," I replied.
"That sounds fat," the philosopher said.

"You could get another skirt," the pilot suggested.

"Stay for dinner," the philosopher's wife put in. "We're having meatloaf and mashed potatoes."

This issue has reached crisis stage in the United States. I know the way I'm thinking about this problem has been imposed on me from without. I can't stand to be dumb and brainwashed about the structure and size of my own body. We will be having further meetings about this matter and I will be giving you reports. One of my characters once said, "I think maybe it is my destiny to start a fad for getting fat."

Then a good-looking carpenter goes by and she decides to wait a few more years before putting her plan into operation.

℆

I'VE BEEN DRIVING along the Natchez Trace, "that old buffalo trail that stretches far into the past." I'm in Chickasaw County, Mississippi, near Cane Creek, moving turtles off the road and thinking about where I'm going and where I've been.

I've been visiting my son Garth, the one that went off to Alaska when he was eighteen. Now he's twenty-eight and he lives on a farm with his wife, Jeannie, and two dogs and three cats and twenty-six cows and five gray horses and two brand-new colts and one lonely guinea hen. There were six guinea hens but foxes killed them so Jeannie and Garth are down to one.

I drove all day yesterday to watch Garth with his animals

and hide out from a lot of sad confused statements being made about me by Arkansas politicians.

I drove to Mississippi to watch Garth with his animals. All his life he has had a way with animals. He can hold out his hand and anything will come to him.

I needed Garth, to touch him and sleep under his roof. He lives in a trailer underneath six enormous oak trees. From his yard all you can see in four directions are fields and trees and skies. Last night the skies were so wonderful — no man-made lights for miles to dim the stars.

The seventeen-year cicadas hatched here last month. Jeannie says it was so loud no one could sleep at night. The guinea hen and the dogs went wild running around gobbling up cicadas like popcorn.

Back in Arkansas the newspapers are full of simplistic versions of a speech I made to the Arkansas governor's school for the gifted and talented. The professional breast-beaters are coming out of the trees like locusts. All I did was tell four hundred fifty students that you had to be able to think for yourself to do creative work. I told them that to achieve that they might have to ignore authorities like their parents and teachers. I was in an especially generous mood that morning and I was trying to show them the full force of my creative self, the part of me that writes the books.

The next thing I knew I was headline news. Thank God for a free press. The stories are calming down and the reporters are printing my side, or as much as I can bring myself to say to defend myself against this tempest in a teapot.

For now, as I stop to write this, I am driving along the Natchez Trace saving turtles in honor of my son Garth's childhood ambition to be the man who builds fences along country roads to save animals from getting run over. I've saved five turtles so far. I stopped one time to save a clump of dirt. A good-looking young man in a red sports car stopped to help me save the fifth turtle. If this was a movie

I was making and the heroine was twenty years younger, I
could have made something out of that.

☯

I WAS TEN YEARS OLD the night the Japanese surrendered. It was
night in Seymour, Indiana, although it was morning on
board the ship where the emissaries of the emperor were
signing the papers.

General MacArthur was there, wearing, I was sure, his soft
cap and smoking his pipe. And General Skinny Wainwright,
who surrendered on Corregidor and spent the war as a
Japanese prisoner. If he was skinny before, now he was
emaciated. Admiral Halsey was there, and Percival, the
Briton who surrendered Singapore. Also, Englishmen, Aus-
tralians, New Zealanders, Canadians, Russians, Chinese, and
row upon row of American sailors in whites. The talks began.
The speeches and translations. It meant my uncle would
be coming home. He had flown bombers over Germany.
Later, he flew with General Claire Chennault and the Flying
Tigers. How strange that the youngest and gentlest of
my father's brothers should have been the one to drop the
bombs.

We had worried about him night and day. Now the
worrying was over. I was in bed with my mother and my
father and the magic eye of the radio was glowing in the dark
and we were listening to the Japanese surrender.

There was no dancing in the streets at 504 Calvin
Boulevard in Seymour, Indiana. My parents were very quiet
and serious. When I said, "Goody, goody, goody, we beat

them," my father said, "Be quiet, war is bad, beginning, middle, and end."

I remember snuggling down into the covers, keeping my elation to myself. Goody, goody, goody, I was thinking. Now they can't come over here and stick bamboo splinters up my fingernails and make me tell everything I know. I had worried myself sick during the war about whether I could stand up under torture. I was afraid they would give me truth serum or the pain would become too great and I would break.

The speeches and translations went on. It was dark in the room but there were stars outside the windows. No more air-raid practices with drawn blinds. Seymour, Indiana, was safe and I could cash in my war bonds. There would never be another war. We had the biggest bomb ever made and no one in the world would ever dare make war on us again. We would divide up the world with Russia and they would run half of it and we would run the other half. Truman and Stalin and Winston Churchill and Ike and General MacArthur would run things and everybody would be happy and have a good time.

The ceremonies ended. "These proceedings are over," General MacArthur said. My father heaved a sigh. We turned off the radio and the magic eye dimmed and went out.

It was some weeks later that Jody Myerson's father came home from the Japanese prisoner-of-war camp. He weighed about a hundred pounds. He looked so terrible I could hardly stand to walk by the house where he was recuperating. "He'll be better," my mother said. "In time he'll be a whole man again." But I had no faith in it. His eyes stared at me through the walls of the house.

I am marked by that war. To this day when I see a group of Japanese businessmen getting on an elevator in New York City I think of Jody's father. I wonder what they think of when they see me stare. It is in spite of such knowledge that I dream of peace.

A LOT OF PEOPLE have gotten the idea that what I do for a living is sit around on a mountain writing a journal. I will answer that, although it is not my nature to explain myself or justify my actions. I do what I think is right and let people think what they please about it. I am not in the business of trying to make people understand my complicated and individual life-style.

What I do is write prose fiction, I write it six or seven hours a day, seven days a week, except for the times when I force myself to stop writing in order not to completely lose touch with the real world. It is easy for me to isolate myself and write books — the hard thing is to live in a real world with other people's needs and desires and dreams. I'm a good receiver — I hear it all.

Anyway, I write for a living. It is an exciting and jealous obsession. One of the ways I fight the obsessive part is by making these journals — they are immediate — out of my immediate experience. Another thing I sometimes reluctantly do is give readings and lectures and very occasionally teach a few days at a college.

But none of this answers the real question. The real question is, How do I have time to write books when other people who wish to be writers don't have time?

I tell students when I talk to them that the first thing a writer has to do is find another source of income. Then, after you have begged, borrowed, stolen, or saved up the money to give you time to write and you spend all of it staying alive while you write, and you write your heart out, after all of that, maybe no one will publish it, and, if they publish it, maybe no one will read it. That is the hard truth. This is what it means to be a writer. I wanted to earn the name of writer for myself and I went to work and did it. I am often awestruck at that fortunate occurrence.

♈

WHEN LAST I wrote about fat, my friends and I were in the philosopher's kitchen trying to decide whether it was wise and/or sane to be so irritated at the body's natural desire to grow larger and to carry stores of food around on top of its muscles and bones. Stores that might come in handy if we lived in a less fortunate country, or if we were survivors of an airplane crash in the Andes or in case the weather should change and no longer favor the great farmlands of the United States of America.

My friends and I have spent many hours this past summer talking very seriously about losing weight. If it is intelligent to give in to the prevailing winds of fashion about how large our bodies should be or become.

How much of our so-called body image is fashion? we asked ourselves. Is it healthy to divest ourselves of pounds? If so, how many? How will we know when to stop?

I am the ringleader of the faction that says, Yes, we must diet. We must to go bed hungry and fit back into our clothes and never give in to inertia and complacence.

So I dieted all summer and in three months I had gained three pounds. Needless to say I do not think this is funny. I think it is very very cruel and unfair.

I was cheered up last night by being taken to hear a young sports nutritionist. She talked to us about food and how we use it and told us about the new studies in nutrition. Telling us a lot of very sensible things about how to become healthy and beautiful without starving ourselves. She kept stressing the importance of complex carbohydrates and exercise and laying off of sugar. The thing she said that cheered me up was that nutritionists are very leery nowadays of people weighing themselves all the time.

We are diverse and wonderful creatures made of starlight

and comet dust. What shape and size our individual bodies take cannot be measured by steel scales and weight charts. We are breathing oxygen created by plants on a planet hurtling through space. We are not a flat image in a mirror or the reflection of a starving model in a fashion magazine. Life is soft and round and generous.

Some of us may be underexercised and over-guilt-ridden but we are not fat. We are wonderful and mysterious and can swim in water.

℞

I WAS TALKING to a reporter the other day and she asked me if I thought my studies in philosophy had affected my writing, shaped the forms I chose to write in. I told her that I didn't separate knowledge into genres or categories because it seemed to me that all of us were probing the same mystery, coming at it from different angles, calling it different things, but all asking the same questions endlessly. Who am I? Why am I here? What are we doing? Is there free will and, if so, how much, and who has it? The scientist and philosopher René Dubos explores these questions with great intelligence and humor. On free will he quotes Samuel Johnson, who said, "All scientific knowledge is against free will, all common sense for it."

I do not understand why I write fiction when the main things I read are books about science and philosophy. Perhaps I think that by exploring character and event I can create actors to act out the questions I am always asking. I have a character named Nora Jane Whittington who lives in Berkeley, California, and who has so much free will that I can't even find out from her whether the twin baby girls she is carrying belong to her old boyfriend, Sandy, or her new boyfriend, Freddy Harwood. I can't finish my new book of stories until Nora Jane agrees to an amniocentesis. She is afraid the needle will penetrate the placenta and frighten the babies.

I created Nora Jane but I have to wait on her to make up her mind before I can finish the title story of my new book. This is a fiction writer's life. Fortunately, I am going to be in California soon and I will drive up to Berkeley and walk around some of Nora Jane's old hangouts. By the time I get home maybe I'll know what to write.

Now I know the answer to the reporter's question. The effect that studying philosophy has had on my fiction writing is that I know that someday I will get to sit down and write a book about Free Will Versus Determinism and the only character will be me.

IN ORDER to be a writer you must experience and learn to recognize and cope with periods of what Freeman Dyson calls stuckness. In order to do creative work in any of the arts or sciences you must go through long or short spells of not knowing what is going on, of being irritated, and not being able to find the cause, of being willing to work as hard as you can and what happens isn't valuable enough, isn't good enough, isn't what you meant to do, what you meant to say. Then you just have to keep on working. Then, if you can bear it, if you don't quit and move to Canada or call up Joe and go hiking for two weeks or quit your job or get a divorce or do anything else to relieve the pain, and it is pain, it's really irritating, it puts you in a bad mood, you are irritable to children and can't focus on anything and keep changing your mind, if you can put up with it and just go right on sitting down at that desk every day no matter how much it seems to be an absurd and useless and boring thing to do, the good stuff will suddenly happen. It may be twelve o'clock at night when you're doing something else or are in the bathtub. It will be when you have given up and least expect it. There it will be, the radium, the formula, the good short story, the real poem.

I have the wonderful feeling that I understand this right now, because last night at ten o'clock a two-month stuckness broke and gave me the best new story for my new collection. I had been reading a book called *The Sphinx and the Rainbow*. A wonderful book about the right and left halves of the brain and the frontal lobes. Very clear stuff about how the mind creates the future. How it marshals its forces and then goes to work at its own speed and in ways we cannot always comprehend until the thing is finished. Very rich stuff. I recommend it for anyone, but especially for anyone who is currently stuck.

MY EDITOR has been here and we put together a book of stories. There are thirteen of them. A very slim volume. Thirteen out of twenty were good enough to keep. There is a story that didn't make it called "The Green Tent" about a little boy and his grandmother who travel all over the universe in a tent. I'm sorry I had to give that one up. I really liked that story.

Hemingway said one of the great problems for a writer is deciding who his audience will be. Do you write for the reviewers, terrified they will call something cute or sentimental? If they manage to scare you enough you will get to the point where you are afraid to write about anything really human, like passion or love. People are endlessly fascinated by love. They talk about it and laugh about it and desire and hate it. Whenever one of us falls in love our friends watch it as they would the progress of a disease.

So I have written a book of stories called *Drunk With Love* in which I set out to explore what I know about the subject. I have failed. Not failed as a writer. But I have learned nothing about love and added nothing to our store of understanding.

"All is clouded by desire, like a mirror by smoke." I thought I was going to penetrate that mystery through my characters. Wrong. All I did was wade deeper and deeper into the mystery. In the end I let the last words of the book be spoken by Nora Jane Whittington's unborn babies.

"Let's be quiet," Tammili said. "Okay," Lydia replied.

God bless my editor. He let me keep that in.

"What are you going to do now?" he asked, when we had finished our work.

"I think I'll go fall in love," I answered.

"Why don't you just go home and stick your finger in an electric wall socket instead," he suggested. "It would save you the trouble of getting dressed up."

He's right. I've changed my mind about going to stick my finger in the electric wall socket of love. I'm going down to New Orleans instead and get my grandchildren and go riding around in my little blue car pretending we are space cadets. I'll let someone younger and braver than I am sit around the house waiting for the phone to ring.

൧

I RECENTLY SAW a wonderful sight. I was driving back from New Orleans and stopped in Pass Manchac, Louisiana, to see how things looked now that the flood waters had receded. Pass Manchac is a famous place on the Bonnet Carre Spillway across from New Orleans. It is a small fishing village that was several feet underwater in the October floods. I saw it then with water all over the floors of the houses and men walking along the railroad tracks carrying sandbags, still trying to save what could be saved.

Anyway, the flood was several weeks ago and I stopped by to see how things were going and went into Sykes' grocery store and talked to the proprietor and had some doughnuts and bought a tablet and a pencil. The tablet was slightly mildewed on the edges. The proprietor told me about filling the sandbags, who all was there and who came to help and we discussed how resilient men and women are. Then she turned around. "Oh, look at this," she said. A great mountain of a man was coming in the door. A beautiful tanned man with white hair leading or being led by two small children. The proprietor told me that the smallest one had been abused so badly he had to be in a full body cast for six months. "That's their foster father," she said. "He's got them now and they're okay."

They were beautiful children. They came into the store and got some candy and went to the back to find life preservers as they were going out on a boat for a Sunday outing.

"Hold me," the small child said, as soon as he saw me looking at him. I picked him up in my arms and held him there. "We're getting to adopt them in February," the big fisherman said. "It's all set."

"Oh, that's great," the proprietor said, and for a moment

I had a sense of sharing the community of Pass Manchac, a
fishing village where people know each other and are involved
in each other's lives and stories.

I am haunted by these events. For many miles down the
road, I was filled with a sense of elation. The story of
mankind is not written in the occasional crazy parent who
will harm his own child. The story of mankind is the big
fisherman who comes along and sets things right . . . the
physicians and surgeons and nurses in some emergency room
who are working the night shift and are there when the
broken child arrives and put him back together and the
fisherman who gathers the child into his life and goes to
work to love him and the proprietor who cleans up the store
after the flood and sells me a slightly mildewed tablet at half
price to write this on.

⚏

I AM COMPELLED to write about this even though it embarrasses
me to keep talking about my grandchildren. Still, this is
supposed to be a writer's journal and if there is one thing I've
learned about writing it is to follow your compulsions.
  Here is what I am compelled to write about today.
  I have been alone for thirty-eight hours with two small
children and no car. I have been locked up in an apartment
with a four-year-old boy and a one-and-a-half-year-old girl
and I am here to report that taking care of small children is
the single most exciting, complicated, difficult, creative, and
maddening job on the green earth.
  Finally, I called for help. That famous seventy-seven-year-
old child-worshipper I have told you about, my mother, is

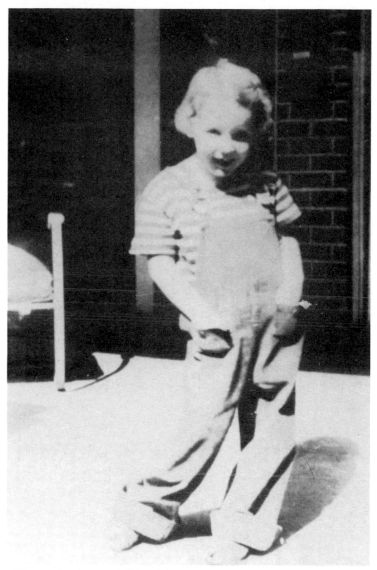

Ellen on sleeping porch, Hopedale Plantation

Ellen on Dixie, friends

Ellen and Dooley, 1939

Hopedale Plantation, built around 1905

Ellen and mother,
1939 or 1940

Friend, Dooley, Ellen,
Aunt Roberta Alford
(Indiana during war)

Ellen and Dooley

Ellen visiting in New
Orleans, taken in booth in
French Quarter, summer
of 1948

Cynthia Jane Hancock
(Ellen's best friend) and Ellen
outside Horace Mann School
in sixth grade. Early spring,
Harrisburg, Illinois

Mother, Ellen, Father, Dooley, 1939

Ellen, 1950

Ellen, seventh grade

Ellen at Columbia Military Academy dance, Columbia, Tennessee, 1951

Ellen at Chi Omega house dance at Vanderbilt or University of Alabama or Southern Seminary

Purple Clarion staff, Harrisburg High School, 1950. Ellen as feature editor

Mack Harness, Ellen,
1984

Ellen at Mardi Gras, 1976

Ellen's sons at her fourth
wedding

Ellen's sons: Marshall Walker, Garth Walker, Pierre Walker

Rosalie Davis, to whom *In the Land of Dreamy Dreams* is dedicated

only ten blocks away, so I called and invited her to come pick us up and go with us to the mall to buy some winter clothes for the children. She's always up for a good time so she came right over and got us and we went to the store. I had it in my mind to buy them some socks and jackets and something nice to wear in case we got invited to a party.

Two and a half hours later the four of us emerged from the mall and began to search for the car. "I'm too old for this," the child-worshipper said. "This is one generation too many."

We had purchased a pair of Superman pajamas with a Velcro cape and a package of T-shirts that might someday fit someone and we had left a children's department in tatters. Only the unbelievable patience of a saleslady named Laverne had made it possible for us to purchase anything.

The child-worshipper took us home and declined my invitation to come in. Later, I allowed the four-year-old to watch a Care Bears movie four times in a row — and that after all my tirades against children watching television. It was a movie called *The Care Bears in the Land without Feelings*. By bedtime he had mastered all the parts and had chosen for himself the role of Professor Coldheart. "THAT'S WHAT YOU GET FOR BEING SO TENDERHEARTED," he kept telling me. "SO MUCH FOR LOVE AND TENDERNESS AND LITTLE FUZZY WUZZIES."

The sun fell below the horizon. We had some cereal and milk. We dressed for bed. The child-worshipper called to see how we were getting along.

"How's it going?" she said.

"How did I do this?" I said. "How did I do this day after day?"

"You weren't very good at it," she answered. "It never was your long suit."

HERE IS my Christmas carol.

The best thing that has happened to me so far this holiday season was a discussion I had at the drugstore with two women who work there. The three of us decided that there was no way we were going into debt for Christmas. No way we were going to wake up on January first with a lot of bills to pay. God bless you, Merry Gentlemen, sell this plastic junk to someone else. You won't sell it to Libby and Darlene and me.

"What do you want for Christmas?" I asked Libby as I was leaving. "I want grocery stores and drugstores to stop putting candy by the checkout counter," she said. "So children scream for it while their mothers wait to pay. What do you all want?"

"I want folks to stop selling dope to kids," Darlene said. "My doctor at the clinic, he's got his only son locked up with his brain dead from taking dope. My doctor was crying when he was seeing me. Imagine that."

The three of us hung our heads over the idea of anyone selling dope to children. We Three Kings of Orient Are. Three wise women at the Katz & Bestoff Drug Store.

Well, this is the saddest time of year and everyone knows it. Adeste Fideles. O come, all ye faithful. Everyone suffers the winter equinox, the death of the year. Everyone knows the sadness of Christmas afternoon after the presents are opened and the dinner eaten and there's nothing left to do but pretend you had a good time.

One Christmas, I stayed all alone on a mountain and didn't eat anything all day while Christmas went on below me. I was the Grinch of Christmas and it was one of the best days of my life. I wrote the last chapter of a novel and wouldn't even answer the phone.

You'll lose all your fans if you start knocking Christmas, the voice of bah humbug cautions me. Not my readers, I answer. My readers are literate people who can think for themselves. They are people who write me letters I like to read and tell me things I want to know.

So here is a Merry Christmas to all my friends and all the people who have helped me make these essays by doing the things I wrote about, and to all the little children screaming and crying for candy at the checkout stands and to all the parents who give in and to all those who say no.

♈

I WENT TO the inauguration of the Radio Reading Service for the Blind and Print Handicapped Citizens of the state of Mississippi. There was a party at ten o'clock in the morning in the Mississippi Public Broadcasting studios and most of the writers in the state were there to start things off by reading from their books. This is a service that will go out day after day to all those who cannot see or are unable to hold a book or turn a page.

It was a bright January morning and everyone looked grand in winter suits and dress-up dresses. The director and manager of the service were there, looking properly nervous and excited. There was an opening ceremony with members of the legislature and doctors and lawyers and actresses and other volunteer readers. There was fierce competition for those spots. Mississippi is not a state where a chance to be on stage is taken lightly.

After the ceremony we all trooped over to the studios and the recording sessions began. Eudora Welty led off with her haunting and beautiful story "A Worn Path." The rest of us were in the anteroom listening on a scratchy desk radio. The minute Miss Welty's soft enchanting voice came on the air things changed in the room and the magic of storytelling was upon us.

"It was December," she read, "— a bright frozen day in the early morning. Far out in the country there was an old Negro woman with her head tied in a red rag, coming along a path through the pinewoods. Her name was Phoenix Jackson. She was very old and small and she walked slowly in the dark pine shadows, moving a little from side to side in her steps, with the balanced heaviness and lightness of a pendulum in a grandfather clock."

Miss Welty was followed by Willie Morris and Ellen Douglas and Gloria Norris and Richard Ford and Luke Wallin and Charlotte Capers and Carroll Case and Felder Rushing and Patrick Smith, some on tape and some in person. In the midst of this excitement a troop of sighted sixth-graders passed through the room with a string of blind and print-handicapped fifth-graders in tow. They were being led by a wonderful-looking little redhead in a plaid dress. She weaved her way in between Eudora Welty and Ellen Douglas and a pair of senators. "Excuse me," she said. "Excuse me, please," and led her charges back to tour the studios which would produce the books they would be hearing.

In a world of television watchers it is nice for a writer to know there is an audience who still needs words unaccompanied by pictures other than the ones they make up in their own minds.

℘

SOME TIME AGO I decided to leave the secluded life where I wrote my books and go out into the world and see what was going on.

*   *   *

I spent two weeks on a reading tour. First I went to Boulder, Colorado, and read a story to the students and had a wonderful time walking around in the snow. Then I flew to Minneapolis–Saint Paul to read a story in the beautiful Walker Art Center. Outside, only a few blocks away, seven hundred volunteer workers were putting the finishing touches on the Ice Palace. In the dead of winter, in one of the coldest cities in the world, seven hundred grown men and women have cut blocks of ice out of a frozen lake and built a palace one hundred and twenty-eight feet high.

Minneapolis is always full of wonders for me. The Walker Art Center was showing the fifteen-and-a-half-hour film, *Heimat,* by the German director Edgar Reitz. It is one of the most beautiful movies I have seen in years. The story of a small German village and its inhabitants from the end of World War One to the present.

On Sunday, I flew home to Jackson, Mississippi, and changed suitcases and drove to Shreveport, Louisiana, to read a story to the officers' wives at the Barksdale Air Force Base. Headquarters of the Eighth Air Force of the Strategic Air Command. I was taken on a tour of the base by two of the pilots' wives. We went to see the sheds where uniformed men were standing on ladders working on the engines of the twenty-five-year-old B-52s and I marveled at the design of the KC-135s that fuel them in the air. I spent the day with the wives of the men who are keeping America safe. Their business is peace, they told me, and I believed them and thanked them for it.

There are many wonders outside the egocentric little cave where books are written. I have found out that the Federal Reserve system isn't part of the federal government and now I've been to visit a SAC base. There's no telling what will happen next.

℃℗

WRITERS HATE to be questioned. It's an almost superstitious feeling that it's wrong to probe or analyze the muse. And yet, sometimes things come to light from questions.

In a question-and-answer session at the University of Colorado I found myself articulating something I have been suspecting for a long time.

How do you create characters? a student asked. How do you keep thinking up new people to tell your stories? I may not be able to anymore, I answered. I've been writing for about ten years now and I have created a cast of characters that are like a Fellini troupe. They are always trying to steal the spotlight away from each other.

It's gotten to the point where it's impossible for me to create new characters because the old ones keep grabbing up all the roles. The minute I think up a new dramatic situation, one of my old characters grabs it up and runs with it. Minor characters get up off the page and take the pen out of my hand and start expanding their roles. Scenes that have no business in the stories sprout like mushrooms as Freddy Harwood or Nieman interrupt stories to give themselves daring adventures or heroic moments.

In a way my characters are right. I can see their point. I have a responsibility to Freddy Harwood to let him tell his side of the story and not just leave him sitting in a hot tub with a broken heart.

Also, I am beginning to suspect there may be a limited number of characters any one writer can create and perhaps a limited number of stories any writer can tell. Perhaps that's how we know when to quit and find something else to do for a living. I live in horror that I won't know when to quit. I don't want to be one of those writers who run out of things to write and then go around the rest of their lives talking

WORK

about writing but not really producing anything anyone wants to read. When I've told all my stories and created all my characters I want to get off the stage as quickly as I can and with as much grace as possible.

SOME TIME AGO I had just finished a draft of a novel and left it in my typist's tennis racket cover and then gone barreling down the highway leading south out of the Ozark Mountains.

I was driving down the highway eating powdered doughnuts and stopping every now and then to write things down. At the end of that journal entry I realized it was an illusion that the novel was finished and I knew very well it would take several more years and two or three more drafts to finish it.

Now I am working on it again. The *Anabainein*, I call this strange creation. A going up, a journey to the interior. It is a novel set in Greece during the Peloponnesian Wars. My pet book, based on a story I made up when I was a child. My mother loved the classics and filled my head with stories of the Greek pantheon and the glories of fifth century Athens, and I made up a story about a slave girl who is raised by a philosopher and allowed to learn to read and write.

All these characters, all this research, all these pages and pages and pages. Perhaps it will be the best thing I have ever written. Perhaps the worst. Still, I have to finish it. A poet once told me that the worst thing a writer can do is fail to finish the things he starts. It was a long time before I knew what that meant or why it was true. The mind is trying very hard to tell us things when we write books. The first impulse is as good as the second or the third — any thread if followed long enough will lead out of the labyrinth and into the light. So I believe or choose to believe.

The work of a writer is to create order out of chaos. Always, the chaos keeps slipping back in. Underneath the created order the fantastic diversity and madness of life goes on, expanding and changing and insisting upon itself. Still, each piece contains the whole. Tell one story truly and with clarity and you have done all anyone is required to do.

I AM SPENDING the winter thinking about money. About money as a concept, an act of faith, a means of conveyance. Also, I am thinking about plain old money, the kind we are greedy for and think will solve our problems. Maybe it will solve our problems. It gives us the illusion of security. Money in the bank, a nest egg, something to fall back upon. Yes, I am going to ask money to forgive me for all the nasty things I've said about it.

I began my study of money by watching "Wall Street Week." I started watching it for a joke. It amused me to see how happy and cheerful the people on "Wall Street Week" always are. No underweight actors and actresses begging the audience for love. Not this bunch. These are well-dressed, normal-sized, very confident people. All will be well, "Wall Street Week" assures me. The market goes up and the market comes back down, but after all, it's only a game. The great broker in the sky smiles benignly down on his happy children.

Why not? I began to say to myself. Who am I to sneer at

all this good clean fun? So I bought some stocks and now I really have a reason to watch "Wall Street Week." Figures appear on the screen, bulls and bears made their predictions. Bulls and bears. Now I know what that means. Bulls are good things that mean I'm making money. Bears are bad things that mean I've made a bad mistake.

To paraphrase a poet, the Dow Jones Industrial Average rises and falls and thy name, O God, is kept before the public.

What a wonderful new obsession. At last I understand capitalism. At last my father and I have something to talk about. Once, years ago, my father begged me with tears in his eyes to take a course in the stock market. I agreed and signed up for a class. Alas, at the very first class meeting I fell in love with a redheaded engineer from Kansas and we went off into the night and never found time to come back to the class. Each age has its rewards. Once I had love and romance. Now I have the Dow Jones Industrial Average and the "Wall Street Week in Review."

I HAVE BEEN OFF at a writers' conference in Grand Forks, in the beautiful farmland of northeastern North Dakota. Where a fellow Mississippian named Johnny Little has just staged the seventeenth annual University of North Dakota Writers' Conference.

Johnny is an old colleague of mine from a class Eudora Welty taught at Millsaps College in 1967. He was born in Raleigh, Mississippi, where he was the smartest boy in town. Then Johnny went to Millsaps and got even smarter. Then he went up to Fayetteville, Arkansas, to make a writer, as he calls it. Then off to North Dakota to teach. The winters were long and cold and he got so lonesome he started a southern writers' conference, which turned into a national, then an international, affair. For seventeen years Johnny has been luring writers from all over the world up to Grand Forks to lend a hand in celebrating the spring thaw.

Edward Albee, James Dickey, Gregory Corso, Truman Capote, Susan Sontag, Jim Whitehead, Tom Wolfe, Joseph Brodsky, the list is long and illustrious. The University of North Dakota Annual Spring Thaw Southern and International Writers' Conference. Not to be confused with the Raleigh, Mississippi, Tobacco Spit and Logrolling Contest, another of Johnny's pet projects.

I had a good time being there but I never worked so hard at being a writer. It seemed to me I was being interviewed or questioned every waking moment by some bright young man or woman. I can't even remember all the advice I gave.

> *To make a prairie it takes a clover and one bee,*
> *One clover, and a bee,*
> *And revery.*
> *The revery alone will do,*
> *If bees are few.*

That poem by Emily Dickinson was supposed to be the theme of the conference but the only time I heard anyone say anything about a prairie was a joke someone told about the flatness of the land around Grand Forks. Nothing to see, and nothing to get in the way of seeing it. I flew home down the course of the Mississippi River and then over to Shreveport, Louisiana, to address the Louisiana Library Association. If you are wondering how I am getting any serious writing done under these circumstances you are not alone. The dour old Scot who rules the roost in my subconscious is very suspicious when I tell him that seeing the world is part of a writer's work.

ᗱ

HERE IS a writing lesson. I'm not much good as a regular writing teacher. I only know things as they happen, at the time they happen. If I knew them all the time I could get up every morning and write a masterpiece. The Greeks got up every morning and wrote masterpieces. Euripides wrote eighty-eight plays, of which nineteen survive. His fellow Greeks liked his plays so much that prisoners could gain their freedom by learning to recite them.

But this is supposed to be a writing lesson. Here is how I write a book. First I get a wonderful idea and I drop everything I'm doing and go and write it down and expand it as much as I can. Then I get very excited and go off and eat some ice cream or something I usually deny myself. Four or five days later I go back and read what I wrote and I decide it's pretty good, but not as good as I dreamed it would be. A few days later the story or characters I began to create will begin to haunt me; they want another chance to show they are as wonderful as I originally thought they were and I go back into the story and begin to work on it. Work means exactly that. Hard thinking and hard attention and walking around the house with the telephone off the hook and the bed unmade. Trying to remember what happens next. It is more like memory than imagination. The imagination part only happens in bursts of excitement — it happens when it gets ready to happen. Days go by while I work and work and work, and, for some reason, which I have never been able to understand, I am able to put up with this very hard, boring part of writing. Meanwhile I take good care of myself. I sleep at regular hours and eat as intelligently as I can and maybe even clean up the house and buy some flowers for the table. The book is writing itself while these things go on. Then one morning, it was this morning for me for this book, it breaks open, like a flower opening or a storm cloud, and it all makes perfect sense and I know how to write down what I have dreamed or imagined. I know what happens next and what the characters are thinking and how they dance with each other on the page. If it is a short story or a poem two or three of these episodes will do to complete the piece. If it is a novel only Athena knows how long it will take or how many spells of hard, boring, seemingly useless work followed by bursts of illumination must go on before the plot is woven and the book finished.

A piece of writing is the product of a series of explosions in the mind. It is not the first burst of excitement and its aftermath. It is helpful to me to pretend that writing is like building a house. I like to go out and watch real building projects and study the faces of the carpenters and masons as they add board after board and brick after brick. It reminds me of how hard it is to do anything really worth doing.

I'M NOT A bad person. If I see a turtle on the road, I stop and pick it up and return it to the grass. I know the universe is one. I know it's all one reality. So why does it make me so furious, why do I want to kill and kill and kill when the turtles on the pond kill the baby ducks? They killed seven in April and five more in May and they are at it again.

Edmund Wilson once wrote a great short story on this subject, called "The Man Who Hated Snapping Turtles." I could have written that story. I wouldn't have had to invent a character. I could have used myself. One morning I wake up and there are five brand-new beautiful soft fluffy baby ducks following their mother out from behind a grass nest and walking side by side to the water. They enter the water without sound. They glide like angels. The mother looks like my beautiful daughter-in-law Rita. The baby ducks are my grandchildren. A turtle rears its head. Kill, I'm screaming. The neighbors are on their porches. They know what's going on. We have all been sharing the tragedy of the ducks.

Kill, I'm screaming. Doesn't anybody have a gun? I grab an empty Coke bottle and run out onto the pier and throw it at the turtle. Success. It scares him off for the moment. Get those babies back on the land, I'm screaming at the large ducks. Don't you know what's good for you? Can't you protect your young?

I can't stand it. Here we are in the sovereign state of Mississippi and we are helpless to prevent those ducks from getting killed. How am I going to travel and see the world? What's going to happen when I get to Mexico or India? Get back in the bushes, I'm yelling at the ducks. We'll drain the pond. We'll kill all the turtles in the world. What am I supposed to do? I can't stay in the house and never go out on the porch. I can't keep the drapes closed so I'll forget the pond is there. It's there. The baby ducks are on the pond and the turtles are coming to get them.

<p

STUCK IN THE very heart of summer in the middle of a heat wave and I'm sitting here trying to write this book. Why did I ever start this book? What on earth possessed me to think I could write an historical novel? I remember when I started it. I woke up one beautiful fall morning in Fayetteville,

Arkansas, and decided I had missed my calling. I should have been a scholar, I said to myself. I should have kept on learning Greek.

I will write a novel set in ancient Greece, I told myself. Anyone can do anything, and I am going down the hill and go to the library and take out every book ever written about ancient Greece and read them and then I'm going over to Daniel Levine's office and borrow all his books and then I'll sign up for Greek classes and I will spend as many years as it takes. I want to be a great and honored writer, a scholar, a serious and noble person.

So I put on my hiking shoes and walked down the mountain and on down to Dickson Street and marched into the library and began. That first month was wonderful. No more the unstructured life of a fiction writer. No more ego. No more taking real life and twisting it into character and scenes and devising plots and opening lines. All I had to do now was sit all day in a little cubby at the university library and read and take notes. I was wearing an old tweed skirt and an oxford cloth shirt and brown brogans and knee socks. My horn-rimmed glasses. At exactly eleven o'clock every morning I would walk over to the student union and eat doughnuts and drink coffee. Who cared if I got fat? I was a scholar now. Lost in the stacks.

Everything was going fine. My time schedule called for me to read and study for five years before I began to write.

I was covering yellow legal pads with knowledge of the past. Plants and herbs, ancient weapons, walled cities, how to mix mortar, how to make cloth, the clothes people wore, their music and sculpture and plays.

Then one morning I stayed home and sat at a sunlit table in a dining room overlooking the mountains and began to read the notes. I was in the dining room. I wasn't in my crowded messy workroom where I am a writer. I was in a sunlit dining room being a scholar. Suddenly an old story I had made up when I was a child began to appear on the page. A story about a young Greek girl who saves an abandoned

infant. Suddenly that old unconscious story, about saving, of
course, who else, myself, came rising up and I was writing
and writing and writing all day.

I wrote for three or four days. That writing is still the best
part of the novel. I may never again write pages as good as
those. And here I am, four years later, on the fourth or fifth
or sixth or seventh draft of the cursed thing and still writing
and still studying and it isn't finished yet.

This is what a writer's life is really like. Calling up my
editor and my agent nearly every day to get stroked and
reassured. Walking around my house blaming the book on
everyone I know and scared to death I can't finish it and
scared to death it isn't any good. "I would never encourage
anyone to be a writer," Eudora Welty once said to me. "It's
too hard. It's just too hard to do."

♉

THE INGRATE, part one, or, I have had too much of the rich
harvest I myself desired. I am sick of being a writer. Not of
writing. Not of the wonderful mystical thing I do all alone in
a messy little room I call an office. Not the inspiration, the
conception, the writing down of poems and essays and
stories. Black ink onto yellow paper, magic. But I am sick of
answering questions and signing my name and being loved
by strangers. "But I am tired of applepicking now, I have had
too much of the great harvest I myself desired."

Maybe it was that one really nasty irresponsible review.
Maybe it is being misunderstood and misinterpreted that
drives writers crazy and makes them go off to the hills to
brood and pout and stop talking to people. Sixth-grade
politics. Fourth-grade emotions. Second-grade sensitivity.

So now I am holed up back in Jackson, Mississippi, with the phone off the hook and the television turned to the wall and I am thinking. I have contracts for three books. I have a wonderful assignment from *Southern Magazine* to go up to the White River and freeze to death camping out with my boyfriend at Thanksgiving. I have three children and three grandchildren, all in perfect health. My new book is selling well despite the *New York Times*. I work for the best radio program in the United States of America. I live in the greatest silliest wildest country that ever raised a flag on a flagpole. And I'll be all right as soon as I get some rest.

Yesterday I was talking on the phone to a writer, and she asked, "Are you writing anything?" And I said, "Of course not." And she said, "Well, that's publication."

IT IS IMPOSSIBLE to be stupid while listening to Bach. There is something about the art of fugue that soothes the brain. I used to make a joke about this and tell my friends they could stop suffering love if they would stop listening to love songs and listen to Bach instead.

Recently, in the middle of a rainy Sunday afternoon while I was lounging around on the sofa in the middle of a pile of books, worrying about my children and getting my mind in a tangle with this or that imagined catastrophe, I came upon a chapter in a book of Lewis Thomas's essays in which he explores the proposition that he could go to the scientists of the world and ask them for the answers to three questions.

The first would concern the strange mind-reading abilities of honeybees.

The second question would be about music. "Surely

music," Doctor Thomas says, "along with ordinary language, is as profound a problem for human biology as can be thought of, and I would like to see something done about it. What music is, why it is indispensable for human existence, what music really means. Hard questions like that."

"Why is the art of fugue so important and what does this single piece of music do to the human mind?"

As soon as I read that I put down the book, went to the closet where I store my records, found a Bach recording, put it on the stereo, and by the third musical phrase the tangles in my mind were unwound and I knew what to do next. The piece I was listening to was Bach's Prelude and Fugue in C Major, perhaps the most beautiful piece of music in the world.

I never did find out what the third question would be.

℞

I WOKE THIS MORNING dreaming of the woods. An opening in a line of trees seemed to lead deeper and deeper into the woods, perhaps to a pasture, perhaps to a river. Tall pine and oak and sycamore trees arching above me and a small road of pine straw and fallen leaves to walk upon, a golden mattress of a road. It was very still, the very heart of the woods, and I was alone there and perfectly quiet and perfectly happy. Some weeks ago *Southern Magazine* asked me where I would like to go in the South, what I would like to investigate and learn about and praise. "The rivers," I answered without thinking, without having to pause to think. Wherever there are rivers and trees I am happy there. I have lived too long to trust the places man has spoiled and changed and bought and sold. They have failed me every one. I cannot even remember the names of the resorts I have gone to with my rich husbands, the sadness and drunkenness and disorder of those places. But the woods. I remember every river I have ever set out upon, every pond and lake and swimming hole, every forbidden borrow pit, every tree I ever climbed or leaned into or loved. "I will go to a river," I told the editor of the magazine. "It won't cost much to send me where I'm going. If only I can find my tent."

"Which river?" he asked.

"Somewhere in Arkansas," I answered. "In the Ozarks. Let me call my guide and get out maps and I'll get back to you."

Of all the people I have ever gone camping and river-hunting with the one who suits me best is a young man from Fayetteville, Arkansas, named Mack Harness. I call him the Trout Fisherman. He calls me the Famous Writer. We get along in the woods. I trust him not to let me get killed and he trusts me to get sullen when he smokes. It's a nice arrangement and we have been camping out and hunting rivers and admiring trees and rocks and waterfalls together for about seven years. So I called up the Trout Fisherman and asked him to come down to Jackson and help me. He flew down and we spent a weekend looking at maps and eating roast beef sandwiches and Oreo cookies and vanilla ice cream. About ten o'clock on Sunday morning, while listening to *The Well-Tempered Clavier,* we came up with something we liked.

"Let's go up here," I said, pointing a finger to a place on a map southeast of Fayetteville and somewhat west of Memphis. "Let's go find the source of the White River."

"Looking for the White," he said. "That's great."

"Where is this?" I asked. "Here, take the magnifying glass. Goddamnit, we've got to get some better maps. We need some geological survey maps. Here is where it should be. Right here."

"That's up by Venus Mountain. We can find that."

"We've got to go to wherever it rises. Even if it ends up being in Missouri."

"When are we going?"

"The week before Thanksgiving. I can't get away till then."

"It's going to be cold."

"I know. Well, you're tough."

"That I am," he said, and walked out on the balcony to smoke a cigarette.

November 16, 1986.

I can't wait. The woods are there and the Ozark Mountains and the rivers so cold and clear and moving so fast. Calm down, I tell myself. They have been there a long time. They'll be there when you get there. And you can make a fire and sleep in your tent. If I can find my tent. When last seen it was in my son's apartment in Fayetteville, Arkansas. It had better be there when I get there *with no holes in it* if he ever wants to borrow it again. What else do we need for a river trip? Some health food. Fritos and Nacho Cheese Flavored Doritos, Vienna sausage and rat cheese and soda crackers and chocolate chip cookies and chewing gum (in case anybody decides to stop smoking).

November 16.

The Trout Fisherman will fly down to Jackson on November 20 and on the twenty-first we will drive up through the Mississippi Delta, through the deltas of the Yazoo, then the Sunflower, then the Mississippi (where I was born) and across the Mississippi to the Arkansas Delta (where the Trout Fisherman was born).

We will cross the river at Vicksburg and ride up the Arkansas side to Lake Village, the most beautiful town in the world, and on up to Pine Bluff, which has been ruined by paper mills and an arsenal for binary nerve gas, then on to Little Rock where we will tip our hat to the editor of *Southern*

Magazine who put us up to this and is paying for the Oreos and Fritos and Nacho Cheese Flavored Doritos and Vienna sausage and soda crackers and gasoline and camera film and, God forbid, the Camel cigarettes.

November 21.

Bad news and a change of plans. The Trout Fisherman has had a death in his family and now will meet me in Fayetteville the Monday before Thanksgiving. So much for our drive up through the deltas, but we've done that before and will do it again in a happier season.

For now I will fly up alone on Monday and we'll find our tent and head out on Wednesday morning. The tent will only be an icon now. The Ark of the Tent. The Tent of All Tents will spend the week rolled up in the back of the Isuzu and we will go find the source of the river and return to spend the night in the Designated Driver's geodesic dome near Goshen, Arkansas, which looks down four hundred feet onto a beautiful S-curve of the river and the fields it feeds and guards. We will sleep near water in this house the Trout Fisherman helped the Designated Driver build. "We are getting soft," I told the Trout Fisherman. "I know," he answered. "Well, that's how it falls for now."

Since we were ruined anyway we decided to get really decadent and spent the evening seeing a double feature. We saw *Peggy Sue Got Married.* Took a Coke break and went back in for *Star Trek IV.*

November 24. Jackson, Mississippi, Airport, 9:00 A.M. waiting.

Leaving Jackson in a hard gray rain. Cold, straight rain with flash flood warnings. I hate to fly in weather like this. Also, I hate to leave my work as I was writing well, working on *The Anna Papers.*

But a writer has to make a living. Also, a writer has to have some fun or the work gets cold. This may be too much fun. Since September I've been on twenty-eight airplanes. Well, two more takeoffs and landings and I'll be in Fayetteville, pick up a four-wheel-drive Isuzu, meet the Trout Fisherman and the Designated Driver, and I'll be on my way.

10:53. Takeoff.

Always a holy moment. We are flying a Northwest Airlines Saab Fairchild 253, made in Sweden, land of the gorgeous Socialists.

Notes on plane: Good title for book, *Principles of Flight*. The Pearl River below me shrouded in mist, wreathed in clouds. So beautiful. Tall pines and orange-leaved oaks along its banks, cold gray water. Eudora's river. She made it famous in the lovely short story "The Wide Net." Also, her character King McClain left his hat on the banks of the Big Black and some say he died and others say he ran away. Rivers. So wonderful to know and love the rivers of your state.

Flying over Mississippi at ten thousand feet in bad bumpy weather I think about my ancestors who came here on boats down the Monongahela and the Allegheny to the Ohio and on down the Mississippi to Natchez and Mayersville. What would they think if they could see me now, daring to complain about anything?

We are approaching the Sunflower River. I can see it below me through the rain. I am wearing a soccer shirt, khaki skirt, boots, and an old raincoat one of my teenagers outgrew and left behind.

Above Greenwood things got so beautiful I could hardly bear it. Small scattered featherlike clouds above a winding chocolate-brown river. The multicolored trees of Mississippi, cold and shrouded with mist, water oak, sycamore, maple, pine, dogwood, and persimmon.

We landed in Memphis in a downpour and let some folks off and took some more on and took off again for Fayetteville. I am getting excited now. Going home, I have promised

John Dacus at Hayes and Sanders Bookstore to be there at four for a book signing. It looks like I am going to make it after all.

5:00: The Trout Fisherman shows up at the bookstore wearing a coat and tie. "I'm ready," he says. "Sign my book." "So am I," I answer, and write my initials on his wrist. [Some people never grow up.]

November 25.
Fayetteville. Tuesday: Cold wet misty weather. One more day and we will leave to find the river. Perhaps the weather will clear by then and we will have a good day for the expedition. The Trout Fisherman and I are camped at the Mountain Inn where the big news is that there has been an accident at the Fayetteville water plant and no one can drink the water. Strange and prophetic that even in this remote mountain town the water is not safe. Too many people in one place. Any Indian could tell you that. The Trout Fisherman is part Cherokee, he becomes diminished when he stays too long in cities, as I do.
When we checked into the hotel the desk clerk handed us each a gallon of bottled water and we carried them to our rooms.

Later: It is raining cats and dogs. The Trout Fisherman left in a deluge to retrieve the four-wheel-drive Isuzu from the repair shop. He returned two and a half hours later with bad news. He had stopped off to shoot pool at Roger's Pool Hall. It was dark when he came out and the lights wouldn't work on the Isuzu. We decided to try to get them fixed in the morning even though it might give us a later start. Perhaps I will get to unroll the green tent after all. I went to sleep dreaming of what we would find. A spring trickling out of the ground, disturbing the leaves somewhere halfway up a hill. Would there be a marker? There was none noted on the map. People in Arkansas are good about leaving things alone. Perhaps there would be nothing there but water. I went to sleep with water beating on the panes outside the windows of my room, falling down gullies and ravines in my dreams.

November 27: Making Our Own Fun, Or, Why Are We Always So Crazy?

5:30: Woke up. Argued about the lights on the Isuzu.

5:45: Trout Fisherman goes out to work on lights on the Isuzu. No luck.

6:10: Called Trout Fisherman's brother. Tried to borrow a truck. No luck. He was driving it to Shreveport.

6:30: Packed Isuzu. Ate breakfast (bacon, eggs, toast, pancakes, hash browns, coffee, syrup). Got in a remarkably good creative mood.

7:00: Drove Isuzu to Jim Ray Pontiac where a masterful service manager understood our problem, mobilized a team of mechanics, and had us on our way with a new light switch in fifteen minutes. *I love Fayetteville.* Where else will people take writing a story that seriously? Where else will people try to save you money while they sell you something? Salespeople in Fayetteville were always doing that for me when I lived there, pointing out bargains, telling me to wait for the sale, helping me curb my extravagant Delta ways.

November 27.

We are on our way. So much water. Rain and mist and clouds, a cold wet misty freezing thoroughly gray day. Perfect morning to go searching for a place where four rivers rise.

We drive out past Goshen to pick up the Designated Driver who lives in a dome overlooking the White River just below Beaver Lake. The Designated Driver is Dave Tucker, an old friend who makes his living as a commercial artist and illustrator. He is also, not incidentally, one of the best jazz and fusion drummers in the Ozarks and played rock and roll with the Trout Fisherman's band in their high school days. It's a good crew. It's going to be a good trip. We can feel it in our bones.

We inspect the river from Dave's balcony. Then we go down the long gravel road and out onto Highway 45, backtrack past Goshen and find Highway 16 to Elkins. It is still misty, gray from horizon to horizon. The only leaves left are on the oaks. We can see the lay of the land, the architecture of the trees, uncovered fences, cows in pastures, red and green and brown fields, barns and silos. We pass the Victory Free Will Baptist Church, Guernseys and Herefords, a field of Appaloosas, their black spots showing on their wet hides.

Near here the West Fork of the White meets the middle fork at the bottom of Lake Sequoyah. "The first dam on the lake is at Sequoyah," the Trout Fisherman says. Later we will learn that isn't so.

We go from 71 to 265 to 68 east, past Sonora, and onto Highway 16 toward Elkins. Between Tuttle and Elkins we get our first glimpse of the river before the dams.

Beautiful country. We drive past apple and peach orchards and vineyards with their black configurations set like Chinese characters against the tilled soil.

Near here, in Madison County, up around Red Star, a hundred little gaps and rises and valleys are the last hide-outs of the hippies, the ones that went back to the land to stay.

Everything in the Ozarks is very simple still. Even pollution doesn't seem to have made great inroads into the beauty. Still, I remember when I first moved here, in 1979, and the scientist Anderson Nettleship, now deceased, would proclaim to me about acid rain falling on our forests from smokestacks thousands of miles away. I felt helpless in the face of that but Dr. Nettleship did not. He protested it loudly all his life, in person and in many letters to the Powers That Be.

Another thing he used to lecture me about was the sheer

idiocy of romantic love. "Childbirth, of course," he would
begin, "is the true manifestation of the creative urge. But
that is another matter." The Trout Fisherman and I knew Dr.
Nettleship and loved to talk with him. If he had still been
manifest he would have made a wonderful companion on this
trip.

9:50: At Tuttle we get our first view of the river above the
dams. Here the river is at its widest, sixty to a hundred feet.
This is the river before it starts being fucked up. Wide green
flood plains, bottomland as it's called in the hills, the
watershed, what the river drains. Near Brashears we pass a
house with white ceramic chickens and a red wagon beside a
well. Perfect and right.

Near Combs there are white cattle against green and
red fields. In the background a stand of white birch trees
against a gray sky. A patch of sunlight beginning to show in
the east.

I have been in this country this time of year when it is so
golden and orange and transformed by sunlight that you can
barely hold the car on the road. Black trees, orange leaves,
blue skies, green moss, still green pastures, the rise and fall
of a thousand hills, mountains in the distance. Dazzling. But
it is proper that today is all gray drizzle and black trees and
gray water pouring over white rocks. This is "water poetry
time," as the Trout Fisherman calls it. Water falling from
the sky, and all around, and underneath where the great
aquifers stretch all the way to Alaska.

A day for mist and rain and water. I am feeling very chic
in my hand-me-down raincoat, wondering if my boots will fit
over my heavy wool socks. (We each have a pair of fine new
socks, a gift from the Tentkeeper when we went by yesterday
to pick up the tent.)

The Trout Fisherman hands me a cookie. He is always
feeding me. He thinks I don't pay enough attention to
myself.

* * *

11:00: We stopped at Fleming Creek to watch a flock of mallards on the water. The bridge over the creek is so old and rickety it's a wonder it held our Isuzu. We walked out across the rocks and stood in the middle of the creekbed watching cars go by, watching the sagging timbers of the supports sway and hold.

"What's keeping it up?" I asked.

"Acts of faith," the Trout Fisherman replied. "I hope it doesn't fall while we're watching." The Designated Driver had wandered off into the underbrush looking for photographs. We stood in the water admiring the sawdust blowing off the top of a huge sawdust mountain beside a sawmill. High hills all around with green pastures, ducks and cows and woodpeckers. Pollution seems so harmless when there isn't much of it.

11:30: We stopped again at St. Paul. Sugar Tree Mountain is visible from here, rising up so high and covered with a crown of mist. We went on, past Slow Tom Hollow and Hawkins Hollow Creek, past Dutton and on to Pettigrew. We had grown quiet, getting near our destination.

11:45: Four miles from Boston, at No Name Knob after Pettigrew. The river is getting very small, lost below its rocky red clay banks. The Designated Driver is driving. The Trout Fisherman is making up water poetry. I am almost asleep and wake just as we go up a hill past a mailbox marked *Love* and there is the Boston, Arkansas, post office, deserted on the crest of a hill. We stop the Isuzu and get out and take photographs. A book called *Married Sexual Happiness* is lying facedown on a box inside the deserted post office. The Trout Fisherman picks it up and smiles at me. The Trout Fisherman and I are always talking about getting married but we never do. We are both too gun-shy and selfish and set in our ways to make promises.

"Let's look for markers," the Designated Driver says and

the three of us leave the post office and start down the hill toward the ravine.

12:40: The Designated Driver and I walked down to where a geodesic survey marker stood up in the blackened leafless briers. The marker was about twenty feet below the shoulder of the road. *WH* it said in large block letters.

"White River," I announced. "This is it." Dave climbed down another thirty feet and found a second marker on a steeper incline above a gully where water runs in torrents in the spring. I had visions of the ridge covered with snow and the sun of early March melting the snow and sending it in rushes to fill the trough. "Oh, yes," I said. "This is surely it." It was all very mystical and cold and wonderful. What had started out as a lark, a created adventure for a magazine article, had turned into a mystery with deserted ridges on gray November days and a lost post office crowning the ridge exactly where it should be. The Designated Driver stood at the edge of the ravine holding his camera. I was above him imagining I was standing upon an aquifer, loving (more than ever) this craziness called Arkansas, a place where men are still free, in the old sense of the word, meaning some of them at least still create and live out their own destinies. Until recently there was a usury law in effect here. No human slavery in Arkansas, no licenses to steal.

The Designated Driver and I kept looking at each other. We weren't satisfied yet. The Trout Fisherman came back across the road and announced that the water came from higher up and we would have to climb. We crossed the road and followed a leaf-covered ridge that curved along the side of the hill below the post office. We could hear water, a steady drip and gurgle about a hundred yards back. Following it we came to a waterfall and twenty feet above that another one.

"Let's hike," the Trout Fisherman said. "Let's do some climbing."

"Let's go to the truck first and get some dry socks," I said. "We might be gone for a while."

"Let's talk to those folks across the road," the Designated Driver added. We left the waterfall and went back to the truck. A red Buick was coming down the hill from the post office. The driver was kind enough to stop and answer our questions. "You need to talk to Mrs. Hunter," she said. "She knows everything around here."

"Is that her house across the road?" the Trout Fisherman asked.

"Right there," the woman answered. "Just knock on the door. She'll be glad to talk to you."

Maybe Mrs. Irene Hunter is just the friendliest and most trusting person in the world. Or maybe it was the pair of long white socks the Trout Fisherman was holding in his hand when he knocked on her door. One way or the other she came right out and offered to help.

The driver of the Buick was right. Mrs. Hunter did know everything. In the first place she had been a forest ranger until her retirement several years ago. In the second place her nephew owns the land that holds the spring we were seeking. She went back inside for a coat and returned and got into the truck. She pointed out directions with beautiful sweeps of her hand. "Yes, four rivers rise on this little knob. The White runs to the north, the War Eagle to the west, the Kings to the east, and the Mulberry to the south." We were enchanted. She was a lovely graceful woman, widowed five years but not the kind of person who gives in to grief. Her children grown and her husband dead, she keeps on living in her house, a comfortable-looking white wooden dwelling across from the deserted post office.

With Mrs. Hunter giving directions, we drove past the post office and up a red dirt road to the crest of the rise. Tall yellow grasses bent beneath the rain. We were all very excited, we were on a great quest and had found the mythical wise woman who would show us the way. We drove through the high yellow grasses and got out and marched along to a small clear pond with a black tree growing up in the middle. "Right there," she said. "The spring starts underneath that tree." We walked out onto a narrow dam and stood transfixed. The dead tree stood up in the water like a symbol. It must have been a proud oak or maple before the first dam on the White River killed it and left its skeleton for a statue to mark the place.

We stood in the cold light rain and took photographs and whispered about the source of water. Not far away, in Eureka Springs, Arkansas, there is a spring whose waters are part of an aquifer that has its beginnings in Alaska.

Below the small dam the water continues down the ravine in waterfalls and comes to the place where we had left our footprints an hour before. Then on down and along its watercourse to where it meets up with the West Fork. Between here and there a thousand million trickles make music and run past the Designated Driver's dome and on to Fayetteville. Then the river doubles back and falls all the way down the state of Arkansas to meet the Mississippi across from Rosedale, where the Famous Writer's father was born, at the beginning of this century, when men still knew rivers and shared and used that knowledge.

We got back to Dave's house in the afternoon and made a fire and heated up the Wok Stew and started talking. It was the best of conversation, about night and the size of the universe and black holes and what fish do in the winter and fish the Trout Fisherman had caught and photographs the Designated Driver had taken and books we all would write and plays we would put on and movies we could film if they would only give us the chance. About the death of rock and roll and the secrets of DNA and how people lived a long time ago and the houses they built and who invented the hearth and what the hearth means and whether the world will end in fire or ice and if we will get what we want out of life in the meantime.

We talked about babies in the womb and ecstasy and

poetry and songwriting and how to catch trout and how to print photographs that will last forever and how the Cajuns put their photographs in enamel on their graves and Leonardo da Vinci and Walter Anderson and Ginny Stanford and the upcoming wedding of Kathleen Whitehead who started wearing her wedding band the day her fiancé bought it. We talked about the hard job of being a young man in the modern world. About how hard it is to figure out what to do for a living and how hard it is to come up to everyone's expectations and how young women are so strong nowadays that a man has to really get cracking to catch and hold a good one. About how to be a man and who to emulate and what to learn and what to know. "You got to know when to hold 'em," as Kenny Rogers sings. "Know when to fold 'em. Know when to walk away. Know when to run."

Finally, we threw the last log on the fire, finished off the brandy, and went to bed listening to the river and the dry branches in the November trees. "Goodnight," I called out. "I love you both. Thanks for taking me." "We love you too," they called back.

Love, it said on the mailbox. What else does a Famous Writer want from a magazine assignment?

ᴄᴘ

THERE WAS a wonderful piece in the *New Yorker* in which the writer explains the Zeitgeist, the way ideas or fads or states of mind spread throughout a culture with the speed of light. All of a sudden everyone has a crew cut or marches on Washington or decides to be very very thin or decides to give up on being very very thin.

I have always been a bellwether of such fads. I was one of the first women in New Orleans to go out running in Audubon Park. I was one of the first ones to quit. Anyone who has ever known me will attest that I have been at the cutting edge of every diet and exercise fad in the United States. All this time I have weighed exactly the same. Except for times when I was too busy to think about my body, during which times, for some mysterious reason, I would become quite thin.

At the moment I have given it all up. As an adult in a world where eating disorders have become a real problem and a menace, I think it is my place to stop acting like a neurotic teenager and set an example of harmony and balance. So all I am doing now is walking a few miles a day and eating anything I want except sugar. Also, I have vowed never to eat another salad unless I really want it and I am having an easy time keeping that promise to myself.

Here is the good news. It is eight weeks later and I haven't gotten fat. I've been eating when I was hungry and nothing bad has happened. Amazing. It is like some terrible spell has been broken. Also I quit weighing myself. I have thrown those damn scales away for good. A steel box with a set of revolving numbers is not going to have the power to ruin or make my day. What a metaphor the body-weight obsession of our century makes. Scales and surrogate mothers and nuclear warheads and mean-spirited people being delighted that young men are dying of Acquired Immune Deficiency Syndrome. I've got about thirty more years to live here, in this culture, with this madness. I may not escape all of it, but I am running as hard as I can. I'm going to begin by learning to love my own little soft round useful hungry healthy body.

FOR A LONG TIME I have wanted to set something straight in the world. There are many people who read my books and decide that I am a feminist. I believe they base this assumption on the stories that deal with an intense sibling rivalry between a little redheaded girl named Rhoda and her brother, Dudley, poorly disguised versions of my brother Dooley and myself. This real-life Dooley is three and a half years older than I am and he was always the pet. My mother liked him best and my father liked him best and my paternal grandmother liked him best. He was always getting his Eagle Scout badge or going to the Junior Olympics or stoking the furnace or carrying out the garbage or being brave when he put out his eye and playing championship golf and football and basketball and track anyway. He went on to father ten children and become a big-game hunter with a reputation for courage in the face of danger and so forth and so on. My problems with him, however, had nothing to do with male and female roles. It was pure sibling rivalry, a bitter battle for the minds and hearts of our parents.

On top of everything else he has done to me he goes on loving me more than I love him, as a Big Brother should. I know, for example, that if I was in a hospital with some terrible cancer and no one else would do it, he would shoot me if I asked him to. He would kill or die for me and that brings me to the real subject of this essay. I like men because they protect me. All my life they have protected me and I believe they will go on doing it as long as I love them in return.

I like men. I like the way they look at themselves in mirrors, quickly, with a sort of sleight-of-hand pride.

I have two brothers and nine male first cousins and three sons and four uncles and a grandson and three ex-husbands. All of them are good-looking and all of them like themselves. Women like them and I like them and they like themselves. They had good mothers. It takes a good mother to make a good man. It takes a woman loving a man to death when he is small to turn him into a man who will kill or die for the women he loves.

I suppose I should modify my statement and say that I like good-looking men who will kill or die for me.

"I don't know what you women expect of us," a philosopher and ex–Vanderbilt football player once said to me. "Goddammit, you expect us to be gentlemen twenty-four hours a day and ready to kill at a moment's notice."

"Yes," I answered. "That is what we have always expected."

It is what we have expected. Down through the countless ages of human life, women have held the babies in their arms while men fought for them. This is not some sort of joke or cartoon. This is the reality of who we are and where we came from. All our modern associations with each other come from that long, indelible history. Once, when my first grandchild was about three months old, I went with his mother and father on a long car trip from New Orleans, Louisiana, to Austin, Texas. I sat in the back of my daughter-in-law's old black Buick pretending I was the grandmother in a Flannery O'Connor short story, wishing I was wearing a hat. I was holding the baby. My son was driving and my daughter-in-law was riding shotgun. We talked about men and women and babies all the way to Texas. It was our plan to figure things out before we got to Austin so the two of them could lead a long and happy life and make a perfect home for the little boy I was holding in my arms. I have forgotten all the things we said or the points we made and argued about and discussed. I remember that we gave up after two hundred miles and decided it was a subject that did not reveal its secrets.

But this is boring grandmother talk and men want me to tell them how beautiful they are and how much we like the way their shoulders grow so wide and their arms so long and how we love their voices to be deep and how we like them to laugh at us and pretend we are dumber than they are. Maybe men don't like that anymore. I know it was out of style for a while. I'm not talking about dumb, like in dumb blondes with small intelligence quotients. I mean dumb, like in let's pretend, just for this evening, or until I get you to say you love me, that maybe you are a bit better informed, able to reach logical conclusions faster, and certainly you can add and subtract better than I can. Otherwise why are you doing that boring income-tax return while I polish my fingernails.

There is another game that I play with my male cousins. It is called I look like a woman and wear this skirt and these high-heeled shoes and so forth but you knew me when and you know that you and I can drink all these bohoes under the table because we are kin to each other and equal where it really matters, in the endless childhood of our shared past.

I love pride in a man. I don't care if it inconveniences me because I can't push a proud man around or make him do what I want him to do or even quit smoking until he gets damn good and ready. I like to see a man square his shoulders and prepare to take a stand. There were all those fifty million years around those campfires after the sun went down and the big cats came out. Maybe power to confront that night is what I'm seeing when I watch a man draw himself up to his full height and tell me no.

Most of my close friends are men. I like women but they hold no surprises for me. I know the good things about women and the bad things about them and as long as they are strong and brave and don't blame things on other people or act like they're sick I like them as much as I do men. Still, the range of possibilities is all within my scope. Not so with men. Men are a mystery to me. I once loved a man who liked to fish. He could stand so still waiting for a fish to bite. It amazed me to watch him fish. I could not understand the patience he gave to it or his delight in the catch or the deep incomprehensible satisfaction it gave him. I think he had been fishing a long time. Maybe for fifty million years.

I loved another man who liked to look at stars through a telescope. He would spend hours on the porch in the dark looking at stars without ever becoming frightened of death and needing to come inside. I would watch him and wonder what he was seeing that I would never see if I looked through a telescope. When I look at the rings of Saturn or the moons of Jupiter all I think about is whether or not we will have to go there to live and if so, how will we keep the children warm.

But I am an old-fashioned woman. I don't want to be a man. I don't want to have broad shoulders or big arms or be the one to go out and fight the big cats or the invading Huns or whatever threatens us next. I want to go on living side by side with men and running my hands up and down the muscles of their arms and worrying about them and talking about them behind their backs to other women.

I can say all that and still know that women are actually wiser than men because we are more intuitive and, of course, much as I hate to bring this up, we do bring them into the world.

I like the clothes men wear. Once I loved a man so much I made him a white cotton shirt with my own hands. I loved another one so much I wrote three books to get his attention. There is an old gorgeous man living right here in Jackson, Mississippi, that I have been loving and fighting with and showing off for since I was born fifty-one years ago. My mother's only husband. My father and I have almost stopped arguing now that he is seventy-seven and I am fifty-one. This is a cause of great concern to a friend of mine who is still arguing morning, night, and noon with his twenty-year-old daughter. "You mean I have to wait until I am seventy-seven years old to get Anna Katherine to be friends with me?" He shook his big intelligent head. "I have known thousands of people in my lifetime and I have always been able to talk sensibly with any of them except for my daughter. Why is that? How can that be?"

"Back to the old campfires," I tell him. "If you didn't argue and fight with her you might like her too much."

"But it's nineteen eighty-six. It's the modern world."

"So they tell me." I reach out and run my hand up and down his arm, not forgetting to give a few pats to the gorgeous breadth of his shoulders. "You can take it," I tell him. "You're tough."

He drew himself up to his full height and invited me to go out to dinner at a place called the Sundancer.

Once, there was an autograph party for one of my books in a bookstore in the same shopping center as the Sundancer and when the book signing in the store was over my baby brother invited everyone in the store to have dinner on him at the Sundancer. He took a box of fifty books with him and sold them at the bar while we ate dinner.

Surrounded by men like that I would have to be crazy not to love men. Women who really love men may have to spend a certain amount of time running their hands up and down someone's arms, but they are almost never crazy.

IN 1985 I was asked to give the Baccalaureate address at the J. William Fulbright College of Arts and Sciences at the University of Arkansas. Wearing a long black gown and a mortarboard and my old handmade leather sandals from the Flying Possum on Dickson Street, I climbed the rickety stairs and faced an audience of friends and students and college professors. It seemed to be the most momentous occasion of

my life but what I was feeling was not hubris. I gathered my
courage to the sticking place and began. Here is what I said.

I am honored to be here. I want to thank the faculty
for inviting me and all of you for allowing me to give you
the last official lesson you will ever have at this
college.
I want to tell you the best things I know before you leave
here. Unfortunately, most of them are in the words of other
people. All my life I have been a reader. Before I could
actually read I used to pretend to read. And reading has
colored and changed my life and made me different and made
me rich.

Several times in my life I have been rich in money, had at
my disposal more money than I could think of ways to spend,
and each time I went out and deliberately got rid of the
money. I got rid of the money because it is a bore and a
terrible responsibility. A roof over my head, honest work to
do, friends, books to read, a small income so I can work in
peace. These are things that money can properly buy. Large
sums of money that allow you at a distance to rule and order
the lives of other people and demand their time and labor
bring their own bad karma with them. And something
worse. They bring fear.
A rich man is always afraid he will lose his money. At any
moment the treasure he so desired may be stolen or taken
from him and then where will he be?

I want to talk to you this morning about another kind of
richness. A richness that is represented by and kept safe in
and passed on by colleges and libraries, the repositories of the
best ideas man has ever had. The poetry and philosophy and
knowledge of the physical universe that thousands of minds
over thousands of years have left here for your teachers to pass
on to you.

The men and women who have taught you, for your sake, and for their own, and for the sake of all mankind, have been attempting piece by piece and bit by bit to give you some part of that incredible inheritance. If nothing else to awaken in you in a hunger for more of this sort of knowledge.

Do not go out into the world and read only newspapers and magazines and watch the unbelievably impoverished and hypnotic junk that is on television. Do not get your fiction and myth from movies and your philosophy and poetry from magazines. It is not only because I write books that I want you to read them. But because I don't want to live in a world where most of the people I pass on the street haven't had anything to think about all week but headlines in newspapers and the stuff that passes for entertainment on television. I have worked for television and magazines. I know how frightened and scattered the people are who make the stuff you are being bored and confused and brainwashed by.

Enough. I swore I wouldn't preach to you. I swore I wouldn't act like you were on your way to the North Pole and I was the last agent at the last commissary passing out supplies for the trip and that if I forgot to give you anything you couldn't get it where you are going.

If you leave here and never read real books anymore, hard books, the kind that can't be read while watching television, then you will be going somewhere where the things I want to give you aren't available.

I spent several weeks walking around my house trying to write this speech. I was getting a lot of advice from all around town and on the phone from California and New York and Jackson, Mississippi.

My mother called at least three times to beg me not to sound like an agnostic. My editor kept worrying that I would talk to you about freedom and forget to say that freedom entails responsibility. A young friend who works for Skyways said she thought maybe it would be better if I didn't write it down but just got up and talked.

My lawyer said he thought I should talk to you about kissing since that is probably the only thing you haven't already been lectured to about and since it might be the most honest and meaningful thing most of you would be doing from now on.

That was a strange and complicated thing to say, and not entirely cynical. My own best idea was to walk up to the microphone and tell you the only role I ever wanted was to be the mother in the musical *Hair* who climbs up on the stage clutching her pocketbook and says, "Now, kids, do whatever you want to do, be whatever you want to be, as long as you don't hurt anybody. And, remember, I am your friend."

By last Saturday I was getting frantic. I never have trouble writing anything. Writing is as natural to me as talking. This is the most trouble I have gone to in years to write something. Finally, I went out and walked around the mountain and decided what to do. I decided to tell you the best things I know. They were written by other men and women. I found them inside the covers of books that were hard to read. I found them and learned them and they represent the true riches of my life.

These things came from books that were the products of long hours and days of thought and editing, visions and revisions, the best parts of the best minds that have ever lived on earth, the essence, your real and true inheritance, that no one can cheat you out of, or steal from you or take from you in any way. As long as there are colleges and libraries and free men this inheritance will be waiting for you and you can come and get some of it whenever you get tired of kissing.

Here are some samples of what is waiting. This is from the first volume of the autobiography of Bertrand Russell. From the prologue, called "What I Have Lived For."

Three passions, simple but ungovernably strong, have ruled my life. The longing for love, the search for wisdom and unbearable pity for the suffering of mankind. These passions, like great winds, have blown me hither and thither in a wayward course, over a deep ocean of anguish, reaching to the very verge of despair.

I have sought love, first, because it brings ecstasy, ecstasy so great that I would often have sacrificed all the rest of my life for a few hours of this joy. I have sought it next, because it relieves loneliness, the terrible loneliness in which one shivering consciousness looks over the rim of the world into the cold unfathomable lifeless abyss. I have sought it finally, because in the union of love I have seen, in mystic miniature, the prefiguring vision of the heaven that saints and poets have imagined. This is what I have sought, and though it might seem too good for human life, this is what, at last, I have found.

With equal passion I have sought knowledge. I have wished to understand the hearts of men. I have wished to know why the stars shine. And I have tried to apprehend the Pythagorean power by which number holds sway above the flux. A little of this, but not much, I have achieved.

Love and knowledge, as far as they were possible, led upwards towards the heavens, but always pity brought me back to earth. Echoes of cries of pain reverberate in my heart. Children in famine, victims tortured by oppressors, helpless old people a hated burden to their sons, and the whole world of loneliness, poverty and pain make a mockery of what human life should be. I long to alleviate the evil but I cannot and I too suffer.

This has been my life. I have found it worth living, and would gladly live it again if the chance were offered me.

Try reading that on a rainy day when you are lonely or a long way from home.

And now I'm going to read you what is perhaps my single favorite piece of writing. It is from *The Once and Future King,* by T. H. White.

"The best thing for being sad," replied Merlin, beginning to puff and blow, "is to learn something. That is the only thing that never fails. You may grow old and trembling in your anatomies, you may lie awake at night listening to the disorder of your veins, you may miss your only love, you may see the world about you devastated by evil lunatics, or know your honor trampled in the sewers of baser minds. There is only one thing for it then, to learn. Learn why the world wags and what wags it. That is the only thing which the MIND can never exhaust, never alienate, never be tortured by, never fear or distrust, and never dream of regretting. Learning is the thing for you. Look at what a lot of things there are to learn — pure science, the only purity there is. You can learn astronomy in a lifetime, natural history in three, literature in six. And then, after you have exhausted a milliard lifetimes in biology and medicine and theocriticism and geography and history and economics — why, then you can start to make a cartwheel out of the appropriate wood, or spend fifty years learning to begin to learn to beat your adversary at fencing. After that you can start again on mathematics, until it is time to learn to plough."

"Apart from all those things," said the Wart. "What do you suggest for me just now?"

I raised my children with that quotation for advice. It's what I did instead of feel sorry for them. *The Once and Future King.* It took T. H. White twenty-five years to write that book.

Here is a piece of your inheritance that was written thousands of years ago by a man named Heraclitus. "All men are deceived by the appearances of things, even Homer himself, who was the wisest man in Greece; for he was deceived by boys catching lice; they said to him, 'What we have caught we have left behind, but what has escaped us we bring with us.' "

Lastly, I would like to read you two lines from Eudora Welty's wonderful, outrageous book, *The Robber Bridegroom*. It takes place on the Natchez Trace and concerns a number of characters, including the infamous bandits, Little Harp and Big Harp. "Little Harp hated to see anything penned up. Anything he saw penned up he would turn loose, himself included." And so, in the spirit of Little Harp, I turn you loose to do anything you want to do and be anything you want to be, as long as you don't hurt anybody, and promise to read some books. Go in peace then, and remember, I am your friend.

PROVENANCE

ORIGINS

PROVENANCE

INFLUENCES